The Gospels

ACCORDING TO

Michael Goulder

The Gospels

ACCORDING TO

Michael Goulder

A North American Response

Edited by Christopher A. Rollston

TRINITY PRESS INTERNATIONAL
Harrisburg, Pennsylvania

Trinity Press International, P.O. Box 1321, Harrisburg, PA 17105
Trinity Press International is a division of The Morehouse Group.

Cover design: Thomas Castanzo

Library of Congress Cataloging-in-Publication Data

The Gospels according to Michael Goulder : a North American response / edited by Christopher A. Rollston.
    p. cm.
  Includes bibliographical references and index.
  ISBN 1-56338-378-0 (pbk. : alk. paper)
  1. Bible. N.T. – Criticism, interpretation, etc. – Congresses.
2. Goulder, M. D. – Congresses. I. Rollston, Christopher A.
BS2555.52 .G67 2002
225.6'092 – dc21

                                   2002003829

Printed in the United States of America

02   03   04   05   06   07   10   9   8   7   6   5   4   3   2   1

CONTENTS

PREFACE

This volume arose out of a symposium in the winter of 2000, funded by Johns Hopkins University and sponsored by the Department of Near Eastern Studies at Hopkins. For some time, John Gottsch had been interested in holding a symposium at Hopkins with the New Testament scholarship of Michael D. Goulder as the focus. The foci of the Department of Near Eastern Studies at Hopkins are the languages, archeology, and culture of ancient Mesopotamia, Egypt, and Syria-Palestine, but at the time, Christopher A. Rollston was teaching an undergraduate course in New Testament in the department. For this reason, John Gottsch contacted Rollston to discuss the proposed symposium. P. Kyle McCarter Jr. was the chair of the Department of Near Eastern Studies during this period, and he pledged his full support to the symposium. Together, Kyle McCarter, John Gottsch, and Christopher A. Rollston organized the symposium, consisting of both senior and junior scholars. Because it was readily apparent that the presentations at the symposium were all very substantive, advancing the field in various ways, it was decided that the papers should be published. Rollston accepted the task of editing the volume. The symposium committee and contributors are pleased to publish this volume with Trinity Press International. Moreover, the support of Henry Carrigan and Laura Hudson of Trinity Press International for this volume has been gratifying and most appreciated. We would like to thank Heather Parker for preparing the indices.

The essays in this volume focus on various aspects of the New Testament scholarship of Michael Goulder, ranging from the Gospels, to the Book of Acts, and the Pauline Epistles. Michael, of course, has made seminal contributions to all of these subfields of New Testament studies. The volume begins with Michael's essay, in which he argues that the Gospel of Matthew was written to be read in short units in the church liturgy during the course of the year. Most significantly, Goulder argues that the Q source, accepted by the majority of Synoptic scholars, never existed. He has often argued various aspects of his lectionary theory brilliantly in some of the most prestigious journals in the field, and the essay published here is a superlative contribution. Bruce Chilton's essay focuses on the feasts and festivals of the Jewish year, based on data from the Hebrew Bible, Late Second Temple Jewish Literature, and rabbinic materials. This is a vintage essay, with characteristic sensitivity and cogency. John Kloppenborg Verbin has been a strong proponent of Q, as has also Robert Derrenbacker Jr. For this reason, Kloppenborg and Derrenbacker have contributed critiques of Goulder's lectionary theory of the Gospels and have done so with both collegiality and forcefulness. Gary Gilbert's essay considers the function of the list of nations in Acts 2, with some of Michael's early work serving as the *Ausgangspunkt*. Particularly impressive is Gilbert's command of the relevant classical sources and his fine discussion of the Aphrodisias inscription. Alan Segal's essay is a carefully argued piece, treating such notions as the afterlife, transformation, and the origins of Paul's gospel, based on an impressive command of late Second Temple Jewish literature, Pauline material, and rabbinic sources. At the conclusion of the symposium, Krister Stendahl summarized the presentations and reflected on their contents. We were particularly pleased that Krister participated in the symposium and that he agreed to have his reflections published here, replete with his peerless wisdom and deft wit. Finally, John Gottsch suggested that Professor Goulder be permitted to write brief responses to the essays presented in this volume. This seemed sage. Moreover, we are certain that Michael's concluding comments will be the subject of future, spirited, contributions to the subject, and to these we look forward.

CHRISTOPHER A. ROLLSTON
P. KYLE McCARTER, JR.

Baltimore
May 24, 2002
111th Anniversary of the Birth of W. F. Albright

CONTRIBUTORS

Bruce Chilton, Bard College, Annandale-on-Hudson

Robert A. Derrenbacker Jr., Tyndale Seminary, Toronto

Gary Gilbert, Claremont McKenna College, Claremont

Michael D. Goulder, University of Birmingham

John S. Kloppenborg Verbin, University of Toronto

Alan F. Segal, Barnard College, Columbia University, New York

Krister Stendahl, Harvard University, Cambridge

ABBREVIATIONS

2DH   Two Document hypothesis

2GH   Two Gospel hypothesis

"Crank"   M. D. Goulder, "The Order of a Crank." Pp. 111–30 in *Synoptic Studies: The Ampleforth Conferences of 1982 and 1983*. Edited by C. M. Tuckett. Journal for the Study of the New Testament Supplement 7. Sheffield: JSOT Press, 1984.

FGH   Farrer-Goulder hypothesis

"Juggernaut"   M. D. Goulder, "Is Q a Juggernaut?" *Journal of Biblical Literature* 115 (1996): 667–81.

LNP   M. D. Goulder, *Luke: A New Paradigm*. Journal for the Study of the New Testament Supplement 20. Sheffield: Sheffield Academic Press, 1994.

MLM   M. D. Goulder, *Midrash and Lection in Matthew*. Speaker's Lectures in Biblical Studies 1969–71. London: SPCK, 1974.

"Putting Q"   M. D. Goulder, "On Putting Q to the Test." *New Testament Studies* 24 (1978): 218–34.

THA   M. D. Goulder, *Type and History in Acts*. London: SPCK, 1964.

MATTHEW'S GOSPEL ROUND THE YEAR

Michael D. Goulder

It is now generally agreed that the Gospels were written to be read out in Christian worship;[1] but it is not agreed how this was done. Dennis Nineham suggests that the preacher *selected* from the book a section on which he wished to speak;[2] but Jews thought that their holy texts were the word of God and that the congregation needed to know the whole, not a selection. Morna Hooker thinks that a Gospel might have been read out *entire*,[3] in the same way that Mark has been performed by a British actor in a single recital, taking an hour and a quarter. This would indeed be impressive, but could not perhaps be done every week; also the Gospels are rich spiritual material and need to be taken in smaller units, marked, learned, and inwardly digested. More recently Lars Hartman argues that the Synoptic Gospels are written in Septuagintal Greek,[4] that is, the style of the Greek translation of the Old Testament, especially that of the stories of Elijah and Elisha in 3–4 Kingdoms (the Books of Kings); and this suggests that the churches read the Gospels in the same way that they read out the Old Testament. Matthew is the most Jewish of the Gospels, and this would apply especially to him.

We do not have any direct evidence of Jewish readings in Matthew's time, but we do have some indications. The Torah — the first five books

---

1. So, e.g., M. Hengel, *Studies in the Gospel of Mark* (London: SCM, 1985), 75–77; M. Hooker, *A Commentary on the Gospel according to St Mark* (London: Black, 1991), 15–16.

2. D. E. Nineham, *Saint Mark* (London: Penguin, 1963), 22.

3. M. Hooker (*Mark*, 16): "It was originally read *in toto*, or at least in fairly large sections"; Hengel similarly compares Mark to a Greek tragedy in *Gospel of Mark*, 35–37.

4. *Viva voce*, in the 1997 Mark seminar of Studiorum Novi Testamenti Societas at Birmingham.

in the Bible — are read in synagogues today in a cycle round the year, by *lectio continua.* If you went to a synagogue one Saturday, you might find they were reading about the golden calf in Exod 32; and the next Saturday they would be hearing about the tabernacle in Exod 35. This system is very old: the same divisions are in evidence in discussions in the Babylonian Talmud between third-century rabbis (tractate *Megillah* 29b); and in the Mishnah, about 180 c.e., we hear that after the special lessons in the month Adar, they go back to "according to their order" (tractate *Megillah* 3:4). Before that we have some possible indication from the writings of Philo, who lived a little earlier than Matthew. Philo wrote two works, *Questions on Genesis* and *Questions on Exodus,* which are divided into books. Ralph Marcus, who translated these works in the Loeb Classical Library, contends that the book divisions corresponded very closely with the modern divisions of the Torah and that these divisions were already in use in Philo's time.[5] But in any case, the importance of reading the whole text and obeying it is deep in Jewish tradition; King Josiah rent his clothes when he found he had not been keeping the laws of Deuteronomy, which he had not known existed (2 Kgs 22:11). People need to know and observe the whole law of God, and they need therefore to hear the whole thing. Two systems of reading the Torah developed, an annual system in Babylon and a three-year system in Palestine, but they were both *lectio continua.*

But is there any sign that the church treated Matthew in this way? Well, again, there is, but it is not very early. Our first account of the use of Matthew's Gospel comes from the writings of a fourth-century Christian pilgrim called Egeria. Egeria visited the holy land in 381.[6] She came probably from France or Spain, and she wrote a detailed account of the services she attended in Jerusalem in holy week that year. She says that the whole congregation assembled in the evening of what we call Maundy Thursday and spent the night in a vigil, processing to the various sites, Gethsemane, etc., where Jesus had been on his last night. There was a reading, a psalm, and prayers suitable to each place, running

---

5. Philo, *Questions on Genesis* and *Questions on Exodus* (Philo 9; Loeb Classical Library; Cambridge: Harvard University Press, 1953), viii–x.

6. J. Wilkinson, *Egeria's Travels* (London: SPCK, 1971), 134–38 (chaps. 35–37).

through the passion story in the Gospels. They returned to the city at dawn and from 9:00 A.M. till 3:00 P.M. venerated the cross. Then on Easter day, they read the story of the resurrection. Egeria also mentions that on the preceding Wednesday the bishop read the story of Judas's betrayal from the opening verses of Matt 26, so that from then till Easter, Matt 26, 27, and 28 have been read in series. Furthermore she says that on the preceding Tuesday he read the whole discourse beginning with "let no man deceive you." This discourse begins in Matt 24, and it is a long piece extending to the end of Matt 25. So from Tuesday to Sunday, the fourth-century Jerusalem church read Matt 24–28 in *lectio continua*.

Egeria is helpful; but she is three centuries after Matthew. Can we penetrate any earlier? We have two hints, one from the divisions in the Synoptic passion story, and the other from the breaks in Matthew's Gospel. It is noticeable that Mark and Matthew divide the passion story into rather artificial three-hour units. Thus Jesus was tried by Pilate at dawn (*prōi*, "early" in our translations). Mark says they crucified him the third hour. Darkness was over the land from the sixth hour to the ninth hour; and Jesus had to be buried by sundown. It was evening the night before, that is sundown, for the Last Supper. After this Jesus and his disciples go to Gethsemane, where Jesus says three times, "Could you not watch with me one hour?" When he is arrested, Luke reports him saying, "This is your hour [perhaps midnight], and the power of darkness." While he is being tried by the Sanhedrin, Peter denies Jesus and the cock crows at 3:00 A.M.

So the evangelists divide the story into units of roughly three hours apiece; and we cannot help thinking how convenient that would be for Egeria's bishop. The whole story seems to be arranged for a 24–hour vigil, with suitable readings every three hours. This seems in fact to be indicated in the Gospel text. Immediately before the passion story, Mark tells the parable of the householder and his watchman, which ends, "Watch therefore, for you know not at what hour the master of the house is coming, whether late [9:00 P.M.], or at midnight, or at cockcrow [3:00 A.M.], or at dawn. What I say to you, I say to all, Watch!" Egeria's church was watching, literally keeping vigil. The vigil was not just a sad memorial of Jesus' sufferings; it was a watch in hope of the Lord's coming.

The second feature, especially noticeable in Matthew's Gospel, is the division of the text into units, usually between a dozen and twenty verses, about the length of a lesson read in church today. In the early part of his book, Matthew seems to signify this by ending a narrative with "all this came to pass that it might be fulfilled which was spoken by the prophet saying . . . ," as he does at the end of chapter 1, the story of Jesus' origin. Matthew often indicates a break by having Jesus move or by introducing a new topic; or he will sign a unit off with a strong closing sentence like, "For many are called but few are chosen." Like other preachers, Matthew is fond of threes: three temptations; alms, prayer, and fasting. The citation of Isa 53 on healing closes a section of three short healing stories (Matt 8:1–17). Matthew likes inclusions, where the end of the story echoes the beginning: "Wise men came . . . they went back another way"; "Jesus was led up to be tempted by the devil . . . the devil left him." In the following table, I divide the Gospel into what seem to be Matthew's own divisions (it is not always one hundred percent clear that the divisions are as I have indicated, but I do not think they are far wrong). There are sixty-four of them, each on a single topic. The fourth column gives the basis for the divisions, coded as follows:

q	citation
o	clear opening sentence
c	closing sentence
t	three subunits
i	inclusion

Unit	Reference	Topic	Code	Verses	Date
1.	1:1–25	the genesis of Jesus Christ	otiq	25	Nisan 25
2.	2:1–12	the magi	oqic	12	Iyyar 2
3.	2:13–23	escape from Herod	oqqqtic	11	Iyyar 9
4.	3:1–17	John baptizes Jesus	oqic	17	Iyyar 16
5.	4:1–11	the temptations	oqqqtic	11	Iyyar 23
6.	4:12–25	Galilee mission with disciples	oqtic	14	Sivan 1
		Pentecost			
7.	5:1–16	the Beatitudes	oic	16	Sivan 8
8.	5:17–32	three commandments fulfilled	otqqq	16	Sivan 15
9.	5:33–48	three Levitical laws fulfilled	qqqtc	16	Sivan 22
10.	6:1–18	three duties	ti	18	Sivan 29
11.	6:19–34	detachment from mammon	io	16	Tammuz 6
12.	7:1–12	the Law and the Prophets	ic	12	Tammuz 13
13.	7:13–29	hearing and doing	tc	17	Tammuz 20
14.	8:1–17	the healing ministry	otcq	17	Tammuz 27
15.	8:18–34	across the sea	otc	17	Ab 5

Unit	Reference	Topic	Code	Verses	Date
		Fast of Ab 9			
16.	9:1–17	three controversies	oqt	17	Ab 12
17.	9:18–35	three healing stories	tc	18	Ab 19
18.	9:36–10:16	mission discourse: welcome	oic	19	Ab 26
19.	10:17–42	mission discourse: rejection	oqti	26	Ellul 3
20.	11:1–19	the works of the Christ	otiqc	19	Ellul 10
21.	11:20–30	the cities and the babes	oqqc	11	Ellul 17
22.	12:1–14	Sabbath controversies	oqc	14	Ellul 24
		New Year			**Tishri 1**
23.	12:15–37	judgment on the Pharisees	oqic	23	Tishri 2
24.	12:38–50	evil generation/true family	oqc	13	Tishri 9
		Atonement			**Tishri 10**
		Tabernacles			**Tishri 15–22**
25.	13:1–23	the sower: hardening	oqti	23	Tishri 16
26.	13:24–43	the tares, etc.: riddles	qtic	20	Tishri 23
27.	13:44–58	parables III: Nazareth	tc	15	Tishri 30
28.	14:1–12	death of the Baptist	oc	12	Cheshvan 7
29.	14:13–22	feeding of the five thousand	oi	10	Cheshvan 14
30.	14:23–36	walking on the water	otc	14	Cheshvan 21
31.	15:1–20	traditions of the elders	oqti	20	Cheshvan 28
32.	15:21–39	Gentiles healed and fed (4,000)	otic	19	Kislev 6
33.	16:1–12	leaven of the Pharisees and Sadducees	oic	12	Kislev 13
34.	16:13–28	Peter's confession	oc	16	Kislev 20
		Dedication			**Kislev 25–Tebeth 2**
35.	17:1–21	mount of transfiguration	oqtc	21	Kislev 27
36.	17:22–18:20	caring for the church	oqtc	26	Tebeth 4
37.	18:21–35	forgiving one's brother	ic	15	Tebeth 11
38.	19:1–15	marriage and children	oqqt	15	Tebeth 18
39.	19:16–30	rich young man	oqic	15	Tebeth 25
40.	20:1–16	laborers in the vineyard	ic	16	Shebat 3
41.	20:17–28	mother of Zebaids	oic	12	Shebat 10
42.	20:29–21:11	entry into Jerusalem	oqqtic	17	Shebat 17
43.	21:12–27	cleansing of the temple	oqqti	16	Shebat 24
44.	21:28–46	vineyard parables	qqtc	18	Adar 1
45.	22:1–14	royal wedding parable	oc	14	Adar 8
		Purim			**Adar 14**
46.	22:15–33	tribute and resurrection	oqqc	19	Adar 15
47.	22:34–46	disputes with Pharisees	oqc	13	Adar 22
48.	23:1–39	woes discourse	c	39	Adar 29
49.	24:1–14	the beginning of the woes	oc	14	[2 Adar 7]
50.	24:15–28	the great tribulation	oqc	14	[2 Adar 14]
51.	24:29–41	the coming of the Son of Man	oqc	13	[2 Adar 21]
52.	24:42–25:13	watch! parables	tic	23	[2 Adar 28]
53.	25:14–30	talents parable	tc	17	[Nisan 5]
54.	25:31–46	last judgment	oc	16	Nisan 7 [12]
55.	26:1–16	supper at Bethany	otic	16	Nisan 14
		Passover/Unleavened Bread			**Nisan 14–21**
56.	26:17–30	Last Supper	otc	14	Nisan 15, 6:00 P.M.
57.	26:31–46	Gethsemane	otc	16	Nisan 15, 9:00 P.M.
58.	26:47–56	arrest	oc	10	Nisan 15, midnight
59.	26:57–75	Sanhedrin and denial	otic	19	Nisan 15, 3:00 A.M.
60.	27:1–26	trial before Pilate	oqc	26	Nisan 15, 6:00 A.M.
61.	27:27–44	crucifixion	oti	18	Nisan 15, 9:00 A.M.
62.	27:45–56	Jesus' death	oqc	12	Nisan 15, noon
63.	27:57–66	Jesus' burial	oc	10	Nisan 15, 3:00 P.M.
		Easter			**Nisan 21**
64.	28:1–20	resurrection	oc	20	Nisan 21

This brings us to my hypothesis: Matthew wrote the Gospel to be read out in church in short units of some sixteen verses each Saturday night; the whole was designed to give readings for a complete year, beginning after Easter and ending at the next Easter, with a paschal vigil such as was still being observed in Egeria's time.

In the right column of the table, I have set out dates in the Jewish year. The Jews have since Old Testament times operated a calendar of twelve moons, as opposed to our artificial months. The moon has a cycle of almost exactly 29.5 days, and in the first century new months were begun when the new moon was seen. But for our purposes it is convenient just to alternate moons of 30 and 29 days; thus on the table Nisan (roughly our April) has been given 30 days, and Iyyar 29. Twelve moons, however, make a year of only 354 days, so that each year the calendar slips behind the solar year by 11.25 days. In order to keep level, the system therefore inserts a leap month called Second Adar every third year or so, which makes problems for anyone writing a text for calendrical use. What the Jews have done is to divide the Torah into fifty-four readings, the last ones being rather short. Then in a normal year they take the last four together, and in a leap year there are enough to go round.

I am trying to set out as normal a year as possible, so I have started from Nisan, the first month, and I have taken the first Sunday (Saturday night began Sunday on Jewish counting) to fall on Nisan 4, the middle position between Nisan 1 and Nisan 7. Easter is the Sunday after the full moon (Nisan 18), and so my cycle of Matthean readings begins on Nisan 25. After that, I simply followed the dates, with the months alternating with 30 and 29 days. The only complication comes when we reach the end of the year. Here I have followed Egeria in supposing that Matthew's church had a long reading, "the whole discourse" of Matt 24–25, on the first Sunday in Nisan in a normal year; when there was a leap year, this could be subdivided to provide for the extra Sundays. In any case an impressive reading was required at this point in the cycle, to warn the church of the possible coming of Christ this Passover. So much elasticity would be required by the vagaries of the calendar. Our sixty-four Matthean units would be needed to cover 50/51 Sundays in a normal year + 4/5 extra Sundays in a leap year + 8 watches through the Passover vigil. Matt 26:1–16 is strongly dated in the text, where Jesus says, "You know that after two days is the Passover"; it is likely that the church met accordingly on the eve of Passover to prepare for its great vigil.

This is a rather grandiose hypothesis; but have we any means of testing it? Indeed we have, for the Jewish year does not consist just of fifty-odd Sabbaths and the Feast of Passover. There are three other major festivals (Pentecost, New Year, and Tabernacles) and two minor festivals (Dedication [Hanukkah] and Purim) and two fast days (Ab 9 in memory of the fall of the temple in 587 B.C.E. and Atonement [Yom Kippur]). If my hypothesis is correct, Matthew must have provided suitable readings for each of these seven occasions.

It will occur to the reader that the chances against this happening by accident are rather slim. We know the themes of all these holy seasons from Old Testament evidence, and we often know details of their observance from later times. If my theory is to be plausible, there will need to be corresponding material for the respective dates, which are now given and fixed in the table. It will not do to provide only *some* suitable readings; for the theory to be plausible I have to provide suitable readings for *all seven*. This is the sort of hypothesis which would have delighted Karl Popper, the philosopher of science. Popper said that vague or elastic hypotheses were unhelpful, because they could not be proved wrong — they were unfalsifiable. A useful hypothesis was one which involved predictions which could be found false. The more elaborate the hypothesis the better; a very elaborate hypothesis, sometimes called a baroque hypothesis,[7] could be quickly falsified if it were wrong. On such an account, mine is a baroque hypothesis.

Our cycle is fixed by the necessity to have Matthew's Passover story at Passover and his Easter story at Easter. Seven weeks after Passover comes Pentecost, which to Jews is the festival of the giving of the law on Sinai.[8] As Moses went up the mountain and delivered the law to Israel,

---

7. J. Rodwell, "Myth and Truth in Scientific Enquiry," in *Incarnation and Myth* (ed. M. D. Goulder; London: SCM, 1979), 64–73.

8. In the Bible, Israel reaches Sinai on the first day of the third month, Sivan, and Moses brings

so now in the seventh unit, Matt 5:1–16, Jesus goes up the mountain and delivers the Sermon on the Mount. Part of the traditional Jewish liturgy for the feast is Ps 119, a 176–verse praise of the law divided into blocks of eight verses, each of which begins with the same letter of the alphabet, with twenty-two blocks. The first block begins, "Blessed are the ... Blessed are the ... ," just as Matthew's sermon begins with the eight "beatitudes": "Blessed are the. ... " Jesus then says, "Think not that I came to destroy the law and the prophets: I came not to destroy but to fulfill; and he goes on to expound the commandments from Exod 19–20, the pentecostal reading. His "fulfillments" take the form, "You have heard that it was said ... but I say unto you." Christians have to keep the laws against murder, adultery, false witness, etc., but they have to do more. The sermon moves on to its climax at Matt 7:12, the golden rule: "This is the law and the prophets." As Moses' law continued to be read for many Sabbaths, so is Matthew's sermon read over seven Sundays.

Back in the sixth century B.C.E., a deputation had come to Jerusalem asking, "Should we mourn and practice abstinence in the fifth month, as I have for so many years?" (Zech 7:3). This fast on Ab 9, during the fifth month, was to remember the fall of Jerusalem, and it is not surprising that the question arose whether it should still be observed in the church. Matthew's reading for the week is 9:1–17, the three controversies: on the forgiveness of sins, on eating with sinners, and on fasting. Jesus remitted such fasts. He said, "Can the sons of the bridechamber mourn while the bridegroom is with them?" "Mourning" was a stricter form of fasting, with no washing or sex, and it is mentioned as such in the Zechariah text quoted above.

Before the exile, the Jewish year used to begin in the autumn; and although under the Babylonians, Jews counted their months from the spring, they still celebrated New Year (Rosh HaShanah) in the autumn, in Tishri, the seventh month. New Year was an occasion of solemn joy: it looked forward to the coming kingdom of God, when all humankind

---

the law down some days later (Exod 19). The law-giving is associated with Pentecost in the (B.C.E.) Book of Jubilees 6:10, 19; 14:20; 15:1; cf. J. Potin, *La fête juive de Pentecote* (Paris: Cerf, 1971), 124–31. Psalm 119 is still used today in the Mahzor, a pentecostal meditation, but its use is testified only from the Middle Ages; see "Pentecost," in *The Jewish Enyclopaedia* (New York: Funk & Wagnall, 1901–6), 9:592–94.

would be judged by him. We find these themes in the Mishnah (180 C.E.) and in the ancient liturgy for the feast (tractate *Rosh HaShanah* 1:1).[9] Matthew has a long reading for the week (12:15–37) that begins with an impressive four-verse citation of Isa 42:1–4 because this foretells the coming of God's judgment to the Gentiles. He will bring judgment to victory, in him shall the Gentiles hope. Jesus heals a possessed man and pronounces, "If I by the spirit of God cast out demons, then the kingdom of God has come upon you." Blasphemy against that spirit can never be forgiven; on judgment day we shall have to give account of every word we have spoken; by our words we shall be justified or damned, as the case may be.

New Year is on Tishri 1 and is followed by the Day of Atonement (forgiveness) on Tishri 10. The Jewish liturgy provides for the taking of a scapegoat to bear Israel's sins into the desert. The prophetic lesson, according to the Babylonian Talmud (tractate *Megillah* 31a), was the whole Book of Jonah,[10] because the people of Nineveh repented when Jonah preached to them, and so their sins were forgiven. The lesson in Matthew is 12:38–50: the men of Nineveh will arise at judgment with this generation and will condemn it; for they repented at the preaching of Jonah, and behold, one greater than Jonah is here. No sign shall be given to this generation but the sign of Jonah, for as Jonah was three days and three nights in the belly of the whale, so will the Son of Man be three days and three nights in the heart of the earth. When the unclean spirit goes out of man, it passes through waterless places before returning, with seven other spirits worse than itself; so it is with this generation. Rituals with scapegoats can have no permanent effect; the unclean spirit just returns with his friends and relations. Only those who do the will of the Father are Jesus' true family.

The Feast of Tabernacles follows, the eight days of Tishri 15–22. Tabernacles is the ancient Feast of Ingathering, the harvest festival; and Matthew's next two units, 13:1–23 and 13:24–43, consist of the harvest

---

9. G. F. Moore, *Judaism in the First Centuries of the Christian Era* (Cambridge: Harvard University Press, 1927), 2.62–63; I. Elbogen, *Der judische Gottesdienst in seiner geschichtlichen Entwicklung* (Hildesheim: Olms, 1931; repr. 1967), 140–49.

10. Moore, *Judaism*, 2.55–61; Elbogen, *Gottesdienst*, 149–54.

parables: the sower with his crop from four different parts of his field, the tares, the mustard seed, and the leaven. But the feast was also associated with the temple, for Solomon had consecrated the temple at Tabernacles (1 Kgs 8:2), and Solomon's sermons, our Book of Ecclesiastes, was read then.[11] We hear already at Matt 12:6 that one greater than the temple is here and at 12:42 of the Queen of the South who came to hear the wisdom of Solomon. But Solomon was famous also for his parables; he spoke of trees and of birds and fish (1 Kgs 4:32–33). So now Jesus tells of the mustard seed which becomes a tree with birds nesting in it and of the fish which are caught in the "gospel net." When he has finished, the people ask, "Whence has this man this wisdom?" (13:54). Wisdom is like a treasure for which men dig in the earth (Job 28:1–12); its price is above pearls (Job 28:19).

Dedication is also an eight-day feast, on the model of Tabernacles, instituted by the Maccabees in the second century B.C.E. after the temple's desecration by Antiochus IV Epiphanes (ca. 167 B.C.E.). It falls about midwinter, and Josephus tells us that it was known as the Feast of Lights (*Antiquities* 12.323–26).[12] Matthew's reading for the occasion is the transfiguration. Just as the divine glory once overshadowed the tabernacle (Exod 40) and later the temple (2 Macc 2:8), now the glory cloud overshadows Jesus and shows him to be the Son of God. His face shines like the sun, and his garments become white as the light.

The last festival of the Jewish cycle is Purim, in Adar, the twelfth month, which celebrates the events described in the Book of Esther.[13] King Ahasuerus is marrying Esther, and she gives a series of banquets, to which she invites the king and his vizier Haman, who is plotting a pogrom against the Jewish people. Finally Haman is unmasked and is taken away to be hanged on his own gibbet. Matthew's lesson is the royal marriage feast in 22:1–14. The story is adjusted to fit the Christian message: God is now the king and Jesus the bridegroom. But there is the same unworthy guest come to the wedding feast, who is cast out into outer darkness to weep and gnash his teeth.

---

11. Moore, *Judaism*, 2.43–49; Elbogen, *Gottesdienst*, 138–40.
12. Moore, *Judaism*, 2.49–51; Elbogen, *Gottesdienst*, 130–31.
13. Moore, *Judaism*, 2.51–54; Elbogen, *Gottesdienst*, 131–32.

Thus it would seem that my hypothesis has survived a formidable testing. Matthew's text not only provides, on plausible multiple criteria, the sixty-four units necessary for reading in a continuous annual cycle round the year. He also provides a suitable — or ideal, I might claim — reading for a Christian fulfillment of the themes of the eight Jewish festivals and fasts. He has the Sermon on the Mount for Pentecost, the fasting controversy for Ab 9, the judgment-day discourse for New Year, the Jonah and unclean spirit passage for Atonement, the harvest parables and other Solomonic echoes for Tabernacles, the transfiguration for Dedication, the royal marriage feast for Purim, and Jesus' passion and resurrection for Passover/Easter. Such a hypothesis may surely deserve the epithet baroque.

FESTIVALS AND LECTIONARIES

Correspondence and Distinctions

Bruce Chilton

Michael Goulder's *Midrash and Lection in Matthew* first came to my attention shortly after it was published in 1974. I was in the library stacks at Cambridge University, pursuing an approach to the Gospels I had begun to follow earlier, at the General Theological Seminary in New York. My interest was in the editorial character of the texts, along the lines of the then fashionable redaction criticism and also in what may be inferred of the character of traditions prior to the emergence of Gospels as we know them. Goulder's treatment of Matthew, a comprehensive argument concerning both literary character and the processes that produced it, naturally caught my attention.

It was surprising that no one had mentioned the book to me. Almost each session with my advisor of the time, C. F. D. Moule, opened with a few routine exchanges, followed by the question, "Well, what have you been reading lately?" In fact, whether at Clare College or later, in his retirement in Pevensey, Professor Moule has kept up the challenge of that question, reinforced by his surprising ability to have read some recent work I have never heard of. My expectation can easily be imagined, when I went to my next supervision fresh from a close reading of *Midrash and Lection in Matthew*. Especially in light of Barnabas Lindars's influential book *New Testament Apologetic*, which built on J. R. Harris's work on the quotation of the Old Testament in the New Testament, often in targumic form, and on the powerful insights of C. H. Dodd's *According to the Scriptures*, it seemed to me that a stream of scholarship at Cambridge had found in Goulder an original and articulate complement, innovative but also supportive of its general approach, somewhat along the lines of Krister Stendahl's *School of St. Matthew.*[1]

But when I referred to the work, a response came which I was to hear many times thereafter. The response was: Leon Morris. Ten years earlier, Morris had written *The New Testament and the Jewish Lectionaries* in response to Aileen Guilding's *Fourth Gospel and Jewish Worship.*[2] So how was Morris a response to Goulder? The answer — as given to me, anyway — was that Goulder and Guilding, both influenced by Austin Farrer, assumed the existence of Jewish lectionaries and their use by Christian congregations and that neither of those assumptions were demonstrable from the literary evidence to hand.

At that same time, Richard France was warden of Tyndale House in Cambridge and had a good knowledge of Leon Morris and his thinking. In addition to reading Morris's book, I also spoke with France about the assessment that went into it. It seemed to me then that Morris's argument might owe a great deal to what I take to be an unfortunate habit among conservative evangelicals. It is a version of what James Barr once rather grandly called "illegitimate totality transfer."[3] By that Barr meant that evangelicals are inclined to insist that, if the Bible is true at all, it must be true in every sense (especially historically). The flip side of that is the frequently heard complaint that any questioning on the historical accuracy of the Bible is an assault on faith itself and implies the general inaccuracy of the Bible. In scholarly debate, this habit of mind often works itself out in the cataloging of all possible objections to a given position, with the triumphant conclusion that if at least some of them stick, the position as a whole has been demolished. Rudolf Bultmann and Norman Perrin must be joint holders of the award for being the most

---

1. Lindars, *New Testament Apologetic* (London: SCM, 1961); J. R. Harris, "Traces of Targumism in the New Testament," *Expository Times* 32 (1920–21): 373–76; J. R. Harris and V. Burch, *Testimonies* (Cambridge: Cambridge University Press, 1916, 1920); C. H. Dodd, *According to the Scriptures: The Substructure of New Testament Theology* (London: Nisbet, 1952); K. Stendahl, *The School of St. Matthew and Its Use of the Old Testament* (Acta Seminarii Neotestamentici Upsaliensis 20; Lund: Gleerup, 1954).

2. L. Morris, *The New Testament and the Jewish Lectionaries* (London: Tyndale, 1964); A. Guilding, *The Fourth Gospel and Jewish Worship: A Study of the Relation of St. John's Gospel to the Ancient Jewish Lectionary System* (Oxford: Clarendon, 1960).

3. J. Barr, *Fundamentalism* (Philadelphia: Westminster, 1978).

frequent target of such exercises (which are, of course, by no means limited to the rhetoric of evangelicals).

Morris's demolition of Guilding's argument represents the considerable skill in debate which evangelicals justly pride themselves in, but also the weakness of that strength. While it is undoubtedly the case that evidence for specific lectionaries in Judaism comes from periods far later than the New Testament, the fact remains that festal worship in Judaism was well established and systematically central until 70 c.e. and well after the destruction of the temple. Yet I did not find any residual feeling at Tyndale House that perhaps the dismissal of Guilding's work (and Goulder's, implicitly) might have been too categorical.

Farrer's work, and Guilding's and Goulder's, cannot logically be dismissed with the laconic observation that lectionaries came later.[4] No major institution of Second Temple Judaism, including circumcision, immersion, temple sacrifice, meetings on Sabbath, diet, the forms of the biblical text, has not been illuminated by collating rabbinic evidence — which all critical scholars accept is to be dated after the destruction of the temple — with the much sparser and variegated testimony of contemporary sources and archeology. And after all, were we really to rule out of discussion the consideration of anything not literally attested in the New Testament, we would not even consider whether Mary was a biological virgin at the time of Jesus' birth or whether Jesus rose in the same body that he died in, two central tenets of conservative evangelicalism which are nowhere spelled out biblically. Critical reflection must not exclude possibilities from discussion just because the dates of our sources are not always what we would like them to be.

Unlike his contemporaries at Cambridge, Oxford's Farrer was what is usually called a high churchman, and his emphasis on the place of worship in the development of both the Revelation of John and the Gospels was unusual for his time and later times.[5] Whether among dedicated evangelicals (such as at Tyndale House) or the less self-identified low-

---

4. This is still the view taken in J. W. Aageson, "Lectionary, A: Early Jewish Lectionaries," in *Anchor Bible Dictionary* (ed. D. N. Freedman et al.; New York: Doubleday, 1992), 4.270–71.

5. See M. D. Goulder, "Farrer, Austin Marsden," in *Dictionary of Biblical Interpretation* (ed. J. H. Hayes; Nashville: Abingdon, 1999), 1.387–88.

church folk of the Divinity School at Cambridge, the whole approach seemed suspect. The earliest Christians might be seen as reading, study-ing, praying, preaching, debating, testifying; but skepticism is frequently encountered when it comes to the assertion that worship played an im-portant a role in the development of the Gospels. That skepticism is not uniquely British (and is by no means limited to Cambridge); the recent *Dictionary of Biblical Interpretation* published by Abingdon offers no ar-ticle on "Calendar," "Goulder," "Guilding," "Lectionary," or "Worship" although comparable topics and scholars are amply covered.

As against that obvious bias, the liturgical structure of early Judaism and Christianity is manifest. The festivals of Israel mark out a deep in-volvement with the agricultural rhythm of the land set aside by God for his people. Each festival is at base a week or so of harvest in spring, sum-mer, or autumn. Spring brings early grain and is also time to move the flocks from one pasture to another. Summer sees the larger harvest of grain. Autumn is the last time of gathering for the cycle, and grapes and olives win more attention than other crops. Although the calendar of ancient Israel developed in the depth of its explanations of these festivals and in the addition of other feasts, fasts, and commemorative moments, the primacy of agricultural practice and experience needs to be recol-lected throughout, if one is to appreciate the sense of the calendar and the genuine joy and enjoyment involved in the festivals.[6] The funda-mental importance of the three great agricultural festivals is signaled by the requirement that every male of Israel appear before the Lord every year at these times (so Exod 23:14–17; 34:23; Deut 16:16–17). That is, of course, an idealized expectation, but it enables us to appreciate how deeply felt was the connection between the rhythm of the fields and the rhythm of God's choice of Israel. It could be felt in city, town, and country, wherever the biblical calendar was known.

The spring festival as a whole — including the Feast of Unleavened

---

6. See F. Rochberg-Halton, "Calendars: Ancient Near East," and J. C. VanderKam, "Calendars, Ancient Israelite and Early Jewish," both in *Anchor Bible Dictionary* (ed. D. N. Freedman et al.; New York: Doubleday, 1992), 1.810–14, 814–20; J. Mann, "The Observance of the Sabbath and the Festivals in the First Two Centuries of the Current Era according to Philo, Josephus, the New Testament and the Rabbinic Sources," *Jewish Review* 4 (1914): 433–56, 498–532; H. Schauss, *The Jewish Festivals: History and Observance* (trans. S. Jaffe; New York: Schocken, 1962).

Bread — came to be called Passover, as is attested by the end of the first century by Josephus (*Antiquities* 17.213; 20.106; cf. his tendency to distinguish the two in his earlier work: *Jewish War* 2.280; 6.423– 24); the historical association of the exodus from Egypt (so Exod 12) is dominant to this day and has been since the rabbinic period (Mishnah, tractate *Pesahim* 10:5). But the term *pesach* basically means "limping" (or "skipping," as some scholars more delicately express the same kind of movement) and referred initially to the limping of the spring lamb (a male yearling), hobbled prior to its being slaughtered, sacrificed, and eaten.

It was a regular practice in Israel throughout the year not to eat the sinew on the inside of the hip (Gen 32:32); the reason for that seems to be that the animal was bound or wounded there before it was killed. The ritual dance of those who took part in the sacrifice could be designated by the term *pesach*, as could the entire festival. Killing a lamb in spring prior to moving on to new pastures produced an early benefit of the extensive organization required to shepherd flocks and provided an occasion for the gathering of Israel, even before Israel possessed its land, and when the name *Israel* probably referred to a series of local aggregations. It is striking that Jacob, a rich shepherd at this point in Genesis, is given the name *Israel* for struggling with God (Gen 32:28), that he is caused to limp in his wrestling, and that his injury is directly connected to the Israelite practice of not eating the sinew on the inside of the hip (32:24– 32). Here we have an image of Israel before the possession of the land: the struggle with God is linked to the consumption from the flock and the blessings that are promised.

The pastoral festival *Pesach* was already an Israelite tradition during the period in Egypt. Indeed, the desire to sacrifice is given by Moses to pharaoh as the motivation for what at first was to be a brief departure to offer in a way Egyptians would find objectionable (so Exod 5:1; 8:8, 25– 32). That departure, in a sequence of events remembered as constituting national Israel, proved to be definitive, and the events of Passover and Unleavened Bread in that sense came to dominate over the meaning of the spring festival, at least for those who composed the Scriptures (Exod 12): now it is God who misses a step when he comes to the houses of the

Israelites (12:23), and the lack of yeast in the bread is a sign of Israel's haste in departing (12:34).

The persistent celebration of Passover as households (authorized in 12:3–4), rather than in the central temple in Jerusalem, reflects the deep roots of the festival, both in the history of Israel and in the affections of those who kept the practice. Under the reign of King Josiah (2 Kgs 23:21–23; Deut 16:1–8), a determined and largely successful attempt was made to centralize the feast, by arranging for the sacrifice of the animals in the temple, prior to their distribution for consumption in Jerusalem alone. The animals at issue now are not only lambs, but bulls as well, in keeping with the more elite institution in the wealthier, national Israel that is envisaged. The temple was destroyed soon after Josiah's reform, but the process of canonizing Scriptures nonetheless favored the tight association between Passover and the temple. As a result, rabbinic practice, established after the second destruction of the temple, does not include the consumption of lamb and distinguishes itself from "the Passover of Egypt" (Mishnah, tractate *Pesachim* 9:5). Still, the possibility of local observance of the festival as set out in Exod 12 both before and after the destruction of the temple cannot be excluded, and even the description of Josiah's reform includes the notice that there were priests who did not eat unleavened bread in Jerusalem, but preferred to do so locally (2 Kgs 23:9).

Passover in ancient Israel was the prelude to the Feast of Unleavened Bread. During that feast, the first grain of the year (especially barley) was consumed without yeast. The removal of yeast and its eventual replacement with fresh yeast carried a practical benefit. Yeast acts as an agent in fermentation, and its effects are passed on; that is, yeasted dough, introduced into new dough, will result in leavened bread. But although the process carries on, after many generations the agency of the yeast is weakened (owing, it is now taught, to contamination by other strains of yeast or by other microorganisms).[7] So yearly renewal is beneficial, a fresh start with new yeast (of proven quality). By timing that removal and renewal at the spring feast, Israel also enjoys its first crop of grain,

---

7. See R. Y. Stanier et al., *The Microbial World* (Englewood Cliffs, N.J.: Prentice-Hall, 1986).

without the usual intervention of leavening. Grain unleavened was in any case the only way in which cereal could be offered to God in sacrifice (Lev 2:11; 6:17), and yeast as such was proscribed in connection with direct offering to God (Exod 23:18; 34:25), so the Feast of Unleavened Bread was a period in which Israel consumed grain in the way that God was held to. Just as the lamb of Passover came to be associated with the exodus, so did the Unleavened Bread. Rabbinic practice (Mishnah, tractate *Pesachim* 1:1–4) emphasizes the removal of leaven within each household in Israel, and that serves to retain the original, domestic sensibility of Passover and Unleavened Bread. What survives within rabbinic practice is nonsacrificial, in that the destruction of the temple makes legitimate cultic offering impossible, but trenchantly domestic, and to that extent it is an interesting reversion to the conception of Exod 12.

Seven weeks after the close of the entire Festival of Passover and Unleavened Bread came the feast called Weeks or Pentecost (in Greek, referring to the period of fifty days that was involved; see Lev 23:15–22; Deut 16:9–12).[8] The waving of the sheaf before the Lord at the close of Passover anticipated the greater harvest (especially of wheat; see Exod 34:22) which was to follow in the summer, and that is just what Weeks celebrates (so Lev 23:10–15).

An especially interesting feature of the range of sacrifices involved in the celebration of Weeks is the specific mention of leavened bread (Lev 23:17). Every major festival occasions a large expenditure of celebratory wealth, but why should mention be made of yeast here, which has been so rigorously removed just seven weeks before? That reference enables us to see two features of both Unleavened Bread and Weeks that might otherwise have escaped us. First, the removal of leaven early in the spring is symmetrical with its reintroduction early in the summer; taken

---

8. As Schauss (*Jewish Festivals*, 87–88) shows, because Lev 23:15–16 refers to counting from the day after the Sabbath, deviations in timing were inevitable. Does Sabbath here mean the day of the feast or the Sabbath after the feast? If the former, which day of the feast would be at issue? Differing answers place Weeks on Sivan 6 (as in dominant Pharisaic and Orthodox circles), always on a Sunday (as among the Samaritans and Karaites, following the Sadducees, according to Schauss), on Sivan 12 (as among the Falashas), or on Sivan 15 (as in the Book of Jubilees). J. C. VanderKam follows this line of reasoning and shows that the dating of Jubilees was also followed in the Temple Scroll of Qumran ("Weeks, Festival of," in *Anchor Bible Dictionary* [ed. D. N. Freedman et al.; New York: Doubleday, 1992]), 6.895–97.

together, these festal practices make it clear that the removal of yeast was not intended to be definitive, but contributes to Israel's usage of yeast through the year. Second, the bread which is specified as leavened is for human consumption. Although the context in which it is presented is sacrificial, this bread is not for divine consumption; it is for waving before God, not for assigning to him in the fire. For that reason, the fact of its being leavened does not abrogate the general requirement that cereal given to God should be unleavened. One of the major points of sacrifice generally is that Israel enjoys what is assigned to Israel and that God takes pleasure in what is God's; together, Unleavened Bread and Weeks show us that yeast was Israel's, and that the appropriate celebration of the festivals would assure the continuation of that benefit.

The agricultural focus of Weeks was so emphatic, there is, as is often noticed, no precise connection made within the Bible between that festival and the formation of Israel in a way comparable to Passover and Unleavened Bread. Still, the Book of Deuteronomy makes the association between Weeks and remembering that one was a slave in Egypt: that remembrance, in turn, was to motivate one to observe and perform the statues (Deut 16:12). By the time of the Book of Jubilees in the second century B.C.E., the feast is associated with the covenant and the Torah as mediated by Moses (Jub 1:1–26), as well as with the covenants with Noah (6:1, 10–11, 17–19) and Abraham (15:1–16). At a later stage, certain rabbinic traditions (but by no means all) would make the giving of the law in Exod 19 the lectionary reading of Weeks (Babylonian Talmud, tractate *Megillah* 31a, departing from Exod 19:1) and would recall that the word of God was split into the seventy languages of the nations (Babylonian Talmud, tractate *Shabbat* 88b). Although the specific association with the giving of the Torah cannot be established as a controlling sense by the time of the New Testament, that meaning grew out of the generative connection between Weeks and divine covenant which had been made long before.

The last great harvest, and the last of the three great festivals, is Sukkoth, meaning Booths or Tabernacles. Actually, the term *sukkah* can also mean "thicket," such as an animal might lurk in; the point is to refer to a rough, natural shelter of plaited branches which would permit the celebrants to lodge in the fields. Grapes and olives were taken in at this time; they require particular care in handling and storage, and sometimes it is prudent to protect the ripened yield. Camping in the fields was a wise practice. Sukkoth, in its material and social dimensions, was a feast of particular joy and the principal festival of ancient Israel (and may indeed predate Israel; see Judg 9:27). It could simply be referred to as Feast of the LORD, without further specification (Lev 23:39; Judg 21:19), in view of its prominence. As in the cases of Passover and of Weeks, the festival was also associated with the formation of Israel, and the Sukkoth were held to be reminiscent of the people's period in the wilderness. But that was a later development, reflected from the time of the Priestly source (Lev 23:39–43), which also specified the greatest amount of sacrifice for Sukkoth among all the festivals (Num 29). Deuteronomy also would have the three great festivals, Passover, Weeks and Sukkoth, conceived as feasts of pilgrimage (Deut 16:16–17) which involve travel to the central sanctuary in Jerusalem, although they were in origin (and probably remained in practice, under various forms) local, festal celebrations. The success of the Deuteronomic calendar corresponds to the emergence of the canon and results in the agricultural year becoming the covenantal year: the cycle of exodus, Sinai, and wilderness was superimposed on the cycle of barley, wheat, and grapes, and the temple (the only place where sacrifice could be offered) became the focus of all three festivals. But it is noteworthy that of the three major feasts of Judaism, Sukkoth has survived best in the rabbinic revision of practice that followed the destruction of the temple. Sacrifice, of course, is not involved, but the construction of the Sukkah and associated practices of festivity make this the most joyous occasion of the Jewish year (Mishnah, tractate *Sukkah*).

Yet in ancient Israel, whether on the agricultural or the covenantal explanation, sacrifice was central to all the festivals, and sacrifice on a monumental scale. It is not surprising that Sukkoth is marked as the greatest sacrifice in terms of the quantity and value of offerings, because it came at the time of year when the disposable wealth of produce was at its height. The underlying dynamic of sacrifice is that when Israel enjoys the produce of God's land with God, according to the preparation and timing and consumption that God desires, Israel is blessed. Sacrifice is a holy consumption, which carries in itself the promise of further enjoyment. Penance may, of course, be involved in sacrifice, but most of the sacrifices of Israel — the festival sacrifices above all — are emphatically understood as occasions of communal, festal joy such as developed countries in our time are for the most part ignorant of. For that reason, the temple itself is a house of joy, and its dedication is crucial. In this context, it is vital to note that, even before it was associated with the period in the wilderness, Sukkoth was named as the time that the temple was dedicated by Solomon (1 Kgs 8:2).

Tishri (during which Sukkoth occurs) is the seventh month, and the temple's dedication then made Sukkoth the time when, in a Sabbath year, the Torah would be read out (so Deut 31:9–13). That is the basis of the later rabbinic celebration of *Simhat Torah* (joy of the law), which closes Sukkoth. The number seven, of course, is basic to the entire calendar which coordinates the feasts, each of which was to last a week. (Although that is not specified in the case of Weeks, both its status as a festal convocation [Lev 23:21] and its name make that probable.) The weeks of the year mark out the quarters of the lunar month, and each week ends with the Sabbath, which is itself a regular feast. (The timing of each major feast in the middle of its month corresponds to the full moon, as is appropriate for a feast of harvest.) The Sabbath Year and the Jubilee Year (a Sabbath of Sabbaths) fit into the scheme that makes seven a basic unit of measurement. So there is a sense in which Tishri marks the new year, as well as Aviv (later called Nisan), the month of the Passover. When the Book of Zechariah envisages the establishment of worship for all the nations in Jerusalem in a new, eschatological dispensation, it is natural that the feast concerned should be Sukkoth (Zech 14:16–21).

During the Maccabean period, the restoration of worship in the temple was accomplished in the ninth month, and the feast which marks that was known as the Dedication, Hanukkah (1 Macc 4:36–61). That seems to have been a popular feast as well as an officially sanctioned festival, but not as important as Purim, a spring festival one month before Passover which celebrated victory over people such as the legendary Haman, described as "the Jews' harasser" (Esth 8:1), when the Book of

Esther was read dramatically and with the enthusiastic participation of the audience. The term *Purim* itself derives from Babylonian religion, which appears to have provided much of the practice and myth of the feast; there was a strong tendency during the Maccabean period to call it the Day of Mordecai, naming it after Esther's uncle, and to assimilate it to the Day of Nicanor, the commemoration of a military triumph (2 Macc 14:12–15:36).

The initial dedication of the temple (and of the system of the sabbatical cycle) at Booths makes it quite understandable that the principal occasion of repentance, the Day of Atonement, takes place just prior to Booths (Lev 16). As in the case of other occasions of penitence, the sacrifice takes a distinct form: what was usually consumed by people alongside God's consumption is now offered to God alone. But the national range of the Day of Atonement makes this occasion uniquely important as an act of rededicatory penitence. After the destruction of Solomon's Temple, fasts were also developed in the fourth, fifth, seventh, and tenth months (Zech 8:19). These are resisted in the Book of Zechariah, but fasting seems to have become an increasingly important aspect of Judaic practice, and it is interesting that what one gives of oneself in penitence (flesh and blood) can be compared to what earlier had been offered on the altar in rabbinic literature (Babylonian Talmud, tractate *Berakhot* 17).

The New Testament does not offer a systematic treatment of the principal festivals and holy days, but it does reflect the deep engagement of the church with the calendar of Judaism. That is easily seen by observing direct references to the festal calendar and other indications of cultic and communal activities associated with that calendar.

Jesus' entry into Jerusalem is likely to have occurred at or near the time of Sukkoth, and the leafy branches which were to be used within the procession of Sukkoth are an important symbol within the scene as presented in the Gospels (Neh 8:14–16 and Mishnah, tractate *Sukkah* 3:1–9; 3:12–4:5, together with Matt 21:8; Mark 11:8; John 12:13). The focus of Jesus' action on the temple, in his occupation of the outer court as a protest and enactment of the sort of purity he demanded there, comports well with the centrality of the temple at the close of the Book of Zechariah. Even his appropriation of property (the foal which he rides into the city; Matt 21:2–3; Mark 11:2–3; Luke 19:30–31) may be seen as an enactment of Zechariah's prophecy, since the book claims that the very horses in Jerusalem will be marked ornamentally with the words *holy to the* LORD (Zech 9:9; 14:20). All this was to be the case because the identity of the Lord as king was recognized, and in the Targum that is taken to refer to the revelation of the kingdom of God (*Targum Zech* 14:9; see Mark 11:10; Luke 19:38; John 12:13). In all of this, the deep connection to an eschatological understanding of Sukkoth is evident.[9]

Naturally, if Sukkoth is a generative element in this complex of material, it raises an obvious question: what is it doing in the presentation of the final Passover of Jesus prior to his crucifixion? That presentation in Matthew (and the Synoptics as a whole) is manifest, so that Goulder's assignment of the complex to the Feast of Dedication may seem strained at first sight. But it is clear that the placement of stories was not invariable within the tradition; John notoriously supposes a different timing within Jesus' life, in close association with Passover (John 2:13–22). I would like to suggest that Goulder's hypothesis is indeed, as he says, baroque, but that it can be fixed. It needs only to become more baroque, to allow for festal connections *prior* to those attributable to the received form of Matthew. The final association with the calendar is not the only possible association and need not be the generative context of a story.

The Feast of the Dedication is explicitly mentioned in the Gospel according to John (10:22). The reference appears in the midst of an extended controversy (ranging over the whole of John 10) over Jesus' self-designation as "the gate of the sheep" (10:7) and God's son (10:15). The controversy over Jesus as the gate is also reflected in the martyrdom of James as presented by Hegesippus, a second-century writer cited by Eusebius (*Ecclesiastical History* 2.23.1–18). In Hegesippus's account, the authorities interrogate James as he stands on a parapet of the temple: "Tell us: what is the gate of Jesus?" James responds with a strong dec-

---

9. In this connection, see B. Chilton, *A Feast of Meanings: Eucharistic Theologies from Jesus through Johannine Circles* (Novum Testamentum Supplement 72; Leiden: Brill, 1994); idem, *The Temple of Jesus: His Sacrificial Program within a Cultural History of Sacrifice* (University Park: Pennsylvania State University Press, 1992).

laration of Jesus as the Son of Man who will come to judge the world. The authorities then push James from the parapet and stone him (he is actually killed by someone with a club, who beats in his head). James's devotion to the temple and his devotion to his brother were coextensive. In each case, the focus was on the throne of God, of which Jesus was the gate and the temple was the court. His court on earth was in Jerusalem, where James continued to offer worship and to insist on that purity throughout Jesus' movement that made that worship possible and acceptable to God. The temple was the threshold to God's throne in heaven, much as in the vision of the prophet in Isa 6. And in the vision of James, the Son of Man associated with that throne was none other than Jesus, the gateway to heaven itself. Devotion to him and to the temple together constituted the effective worship of God. Loyalty to Jesus and loyalty to the temple both demanded rigorous attention to the issue of holiness, of what belongs to God in human comportment. John 10, together with Hegesippus's portrayal of James and his martyrdom, provide insight into the worship of what was in its time the most influential and public expression of faith in Jesus.

It is fascinating that the issue of Jesus' status as divine Son features at the start of the run of material in Matt 17:5 that Goulder assigns to the Dedication and also in the dispute that follows Jesus' discourse in John 10:35–36. Of course, in both cases we would be dealing with a distinctively Christian reading of what the Feast of Dedication involves and therefore with a secondary context, but the possible affinity remains evocative, and the evocations which Goulder's work facilitates, in my judgment, make it well worth reading and pondering.

Such is the dominance of Passover within the calendar of Christianity that Purim has little echo. Still, Herod Antipas is pictured in Mark 6:23 as promising up to half his kingdom to little Salome (as she is called in Josephus, *Antiquities* 18.136), which is just what Ahasuerus repeatedly promises Esther (Esth 5:3, 6; 7:2). Of course, the events concerning John the Baptist's beheading are not Purim, but a terrible reversal of the heroism of Esther. Salome's famous dance and its result represent an antithesis of the themes of Purim. Although all the elements of the legend cannot be proven to be fictional, in aggregate their purpose is to exculpate Antipas from what only Antipas could be responsible for (John's death). There is an obvious analogy with the treatment of Pilate in the Gospels, where he is made to seem the dupe of the system that he was in fact in charge of. In any case, it is notable that Luke's Antipas is more vigorous (Luke 3:19–20; 9:7–9) and makes his decision quite literally without the song and dance: Salome makes no appearance in Luke.

Salome does appear in Matthew, but Herod does not promise her up to half his kingdom, just whatever she might ask (Matt 14:7). In that sense, the story is not treated as a *Purimspiel* at all, so that liturgical reassignment is plausible, although the connection with Sukkoth seems tenuous, and I notice that Goulder cites only the opening phrase and the closing phrase to justify inclusion within the unit.

The influence of James and his circle is by no means limited to the Feast of the Dedication. The most distinctive appropriation of a Judaic festival within the church was occasioned by Passover. Although the Gospel according to John presents Jesus' death at the time the paschal lambs were slain (John 19:14, 31), the Synoptics imagine that the Last Supper was a Seder, the meal of Passover (Matt 26:17–20; Mark 14:12–17; Luke 22:7–14). There are several reasons for which this identification is implausible. No mention is made in the account of the supper of the lamb, the bitter herbs, the unleavened bread, or the exodus from Egypt, all of which are prescribed in Exod 12. Moreover, the cultic authorities are presented as solemnly deciding to act in the case of Jesus before the feast itself (Matt 26:3–5; Mark 14:1–2). It seems clear that Jesus died near the time of Passover (having entered Jerusalem at or near Sukkoth), and that this timing then became coordinated with the Passover itself within the practice of the church.[10]

The later history of the church permits us to understand the development and the theology of this practice. During the second century, a serious crisis concerning the calendar divided Christians (Eusebius, *Ecclesiastical History* 5.23–24). Most celebrated Easter on Sunday, the Lord's day, and chose the Sunday following the time of Passover. Others,

---

10. The consideration of these questions necessitates a thorough scrutiny of the development of Eucharist within primitive Christianity; see Chilton, *Feast of Meanings*.

chiefly in Asia Minor, followed what they said was an ancient tradition and broke the fast prior to Easter only on Nisan 14, the day the lambs of Passover were to be slain and then consumed at evening (the start of Nisan 15). Further, they claimed that this corresponded to the move-ment of the heavenly bodies, in that Passover fell precisely on the first full moon after the vernal equinox (as Passover was regularly calculated).

Here we have a tradition for the precise keeping of Passover connected with astronomy. Astronomical and calendrical observance is precisely what Paul attacks in Galatians as part of the program of the group he considers an artificial Judaizing (Gal 4:9–10; cf. 2:14). Chief among his disputants are followers of James (2:12). But the principal point of contention between Paul and Judaizers is the necessity of circumcision (2:3–10; 5:6–12; 6:12–16). James himself seems not to have required circumcision of all believers; that is, he granted that non-Jews could be baptized and as such were to be acknowledged as saved by Jesus (so Acts 15:13–21). But by presenting the Last Supper as a Seder, James and his circle assured that the leadership of the church would be Judaic in character, because Exodus itself stipulated that only the circumcised, whether Israelites or not, were to eat of the paschal meal (Exod 12:48).

Goulder's assignment of this complex to Passover, then, strikes me as thoroughly plausible. But it is striking that his criteria of selection do not permit him to observe the deepest link to Passover of them all: this story actually names the feast and refers to practical preparation for it.

Just as the influence of James and his circle is greatest in connection with Passover, Weeks (Pentecost) is the most notable contribution (in calendrical terms) of Peter and his circle. The timing of the coming of the Holy Spirit is unequivocal (Acts 2:1–4), and the theme of Moses' dispensing of the spirit on his elders is reflected (Num 11:11–29). The association of Weeks with the covenant with Noah may help to explain why the coming of the Spirit then was to extend to humanity at large (Acts 2:5–11). Firstfruits was celebrated at Weeks (Num 28:26) and expressed the gift of spirit and resurrection in Paul's theology (Rom 8:23; 11:16; 1 Cor 15:20, 23). We should expect such connections with the pentecostal theology of Peter in one of Peter's students (Gal 1:18), as we should expect him to be especially concerned to keep the Feast of

Pentecost (1 Cor 16:8; Acts 20:16) despite what he said about calendrical observations in Galatians.

The assignment of the most law-oriented teachings of Jesus to a pentecostal period by Goulder is plausible, but it should also be observed that the transfiguration, which puts Jesus into direct contact with Moses and Elijah, carries out the covenantal motif of the Feast of Weeks. Moreover, the vision of God's throne, the *merkabah*, is a Pentecost lection in the Babylonian Talmud (tractate *Megillah* 31a, where the first alternative is Hab 3), a perfect supplement to Moses' vision of that throne mentioned in Exod 24:10 and realized again in the transfiguration.[11]

As the Feast of Purim finds itself inverted in the presentation of Mark, so the destruction of the temple is treated, not as an occasion of mourning, but as the culmination of apocalyptic prophecy in Matt 24–25; Mark 13; Luke 21. In rabbinic Judaism, the destruction of the temple was remembered on Ab 9 (the fifth month, corresponding mostly to our August), an apparent compromise between the recollection of the destruction of the First Temple on Ab 7 (2 Kgs 25:8) and of the Second Temple on Ab 10 (so Josephus, *Jewish War* 6.250).

The destruction of the temple also had a signal impact on the understanding of the Day of Atonement in both Judaism and Christianity. Tractate *Yoma* 1:1–5:7 in the Mishnah rehearses the meticulous preparations for that great occasion in anticipation that the temple would function again. In Heb 9:1–12 all the elements of sacrifice, temple, and priesthood are understood only to have foreshadowed the perfect offering of Christ, once for all. The appropriation of the Judaic festal and penitential calendar was not merely a matter of replication. Throughout the New Testament, from Jesus to the author of Hebrews, the evident conviction is reflected that Israel's time, a time of celebrating divine providence in nature and in history, had become final time, the moment of eschatological fulfillment. For that reason, the shift of the target of Purim, from Haman to the temple, as Goulder supposes, seems possible, although it does involve quite a reversal of the themes of Purim and Ab 9. The technique seems more like typology than midrash, and the

---

11. See B. Chilton, "Transfiguration," in *Anchor Bible Dictionary* (ed. D. N. Freedman et al.; New York: Doubleday, 1992), 6.640–42.

theology more supersessionist than Judaic. But then this is the Gospel that asserts Jewish bloodguilt for Jesus' death (Matt 27:25).

Two related issues emerge when I consider Goulder's scheme through the lens of the festal calendar of Judaism. First, the plausibility of liturgical influence becomes plain. But at the same time, I have repeatedly called attention to the ways in which the pericopes I have referred to could easily have been associated with other calendrical moments. The hypothesis is presently baroque in its breadth, and in my view it should become so in its depth, as well. The second issue follows from the first. Consistently and openly, Goulder has stressed the single mind of the author as the fashioner of the Gospel. That continues Farrer's skepticism about the kind of form and source criticism which divides up the text until there is no meaning left, and today Goulder's work is a welcome shelter against postmodernist jargon in literary criticism. But having said that, I would also close with the observation that festivals and lectionaries are not usually the work of heroic authors. They typically evolve within communities, layering meanings and practices over time. That would help to explain the present complexity of meaning in Matthew (as well as in the other Gospels). Absent such an explanation, we would have to conclude that any single author of the first Gospel had to have been every bit as clever as Michael Goulder himself is. And that I find implausible.

THREE

GOULDER AND
THE NEW PARADIGM

A Critical Appreciation of Michael Goulder
on the Synoptic Problem

John S. Kloppenborg Verbin

My first meeting with Michael Goulder was at the 1980 meeting of the
Studiorum Novi Testamenti Societas in Toronto, but my first encounter
was in 1975 when I had just begun graduate studies with a course on
Matthean redaction, offered by one of Rudolph Schnackenburg's *Doktor-
kinder*. Needless to say, perhaps, Goulder's *Midrash and Lection in Matthew*
was not on the reading list. Nevertheless, I stumbled upon it in the
library, read it, and although he did not persuade me of his Mark-
without-Q world, he had a wealth of important and helpful insights
into Matthew's editorial procedures. When I related some of these to
my mentor, I vaguely realized that I had stumbled into the realm of
heresy. Würzburg and Birmingham were evidently farther removed from
one another than Birmingham and Toronto.

It was when I began teaching a regular doctoral seminar on the Synoptic Problem that I came to appreciate Goulder's contribution — second
only to William R. Farmer's — in keeping the Synoptic Problem a vital
issue. I fear that this essay might seem a shade more critical than ap-
preciative, but it is offered here in the spirit of the serious and careful
discussion that characterizes Goulder's own works.

Two scholars have been responsible in large measure for keeping the
Synoptic Problem an interesting and debated issue, William R. Farmer

(along with the team of scholars he has assembled) and Michael Goulder. Farmer's 1964 volume *The Synoptic Problem* surveyed scholarship on the Synoptic Problem from Lessing and Griesbach to B. H. Streeter, pointing out the places where proponents of various source theories drew fallacious conclusions, where they failed to consider fully the merits of alternate solutions, or where they engaged in spurious argumentation.[1] Critical of the consensus that had formed in the late nineteenth century around the Two Document hypothesis (2DH), Farmer offered a defense of the Owen-Griesbach hypothesis, which suggested that Matthew was the first Gospel, that Luke used Matthew directly, and that Mark conflated Matthew and Luke.[2] A decade later, Goulder revived a theory of Austin Farrer,[3] which, like the 2DH, maintained Markan priority and Matthew's use of Mark, but which, like Griesbach, posited Luke's direct dependence on Matthew. This obviated the need to posit a sayings source, since Luke's double tradition material came directly from Matthew. Goulder developed this interesting thesis in two major monographs (*MLM; LNP*) and a long series of journal articles.[4]

Goulder's thesis has eight components (adapted from *LNP* 22–23):

---

1. W. R. Farmer, *The Synoptic Problem: A Critical Analysis* (New York: Macmillan, 1964; repr. Dillsboro: Western North Carolina Press, 1976).

2. The hypothesis now goes by the name Two Gospel hypothesis (2GH). The research team assembled by Farmer has published a defense of Luke's treatment of Matthew on the 2GH: A. J. McNicol, D. L. Dungan, and D. B. Peabody, *Beyond the Q Impasse — Luke's Use of Matthew: A Demonstration by the Research Team of the International Institute for Gospel Studies* (Valley Forge, Pa.: Trinity, 1996); and will soon publish an account of Mark's conflation of Matthew and Luke.

3. A. M. Farrer, "On Dispensing with Q," in *Studies in the Gospels in Memory of R. H. Lightfoot* (ed. D. E. Nineham; Oxford: Blackwell, 1955), 57–88; repr. in *The Two-Source Hypothesis: A Critical Appraisal* (ed. A. J. Bellinzoni; Macon, Ga.: Mercer University Press, 1985), 321–56.

4. "St. Luke's Genesis" (with M. L. Sanderson), *Journal of Theological Studies* n.s. 8 (1957): 12–30; "The Composition of the Lord's Prayer," *Journal of Theological Studies* n.s. 14 (1964): 32–45; "Characteristics of the Parables in the Several Parables," *Journal of Theological Studies* n.s. 19 (1968): 51–69; "Putting Q"; "Mark xvi.1–8 and Parallels," *New Testament Studies* 24 (1978): 235–40; "Farrer on Q," *Theology* 83 (1980): 190–95; "Some Observations on Professor Farmer's 'Certain Results,'" in *Synoptic Studies: The Ampleforth Conferences of 1982 and 1983* (ed. C. M. Tuckett; Journal for the Study of the New Testament Supplement 7; Sheffield: JSOT Press, 1984), 99–104 (Farmer's reply on 105–9); "Crank"; "A House Built on Sand," in *Alternative Approaches to New Testament Study* (ed. A. E. Harvey; London: SPCK, 1985), 1–24; "Luke's Compositional Options," *New Testament Studies* 39 (1993): 150–52; "Luke's Knowledge of Matthew," in *Minor Agreements: Symposium Göttingen 1991* (ed. G. Strecker; Göttinger theologische Arbeiten 50; Göttingen: Vandenhoeck & Ruprecht, 1993), 143–60; "The Pre-Marcan Gospel," *Scottish Journal of Theology* 47 (1994): 453–71; "Juggernaut"; "Self-Contradiction in the IQP?" *Journal of Biblical Literature* 118 (1999): 506–17.

1. Part of Mark is based on reliable Jesus tradition; it is doubtful, however, that such is present in the non-Markan sections of the other Gospels.

2. Markan traditions were collected and transmitted by the Jerusalem community under Peter, James, and John, who amplified and eroded them.

3. These traditions were written by Mark approximately 70 c.e., with further editorial additions and attenuations.

4. There is no other collection of sayings, such as Q.

5. Matthew wrote his Gospel approximately 80 c.e. as an expansion of Mark for a Jewish-Christian community. Matthew was a highly creative author, elaborating Mark freely, (largely) without dependence on other tradition, oral or written. Matthew's Gospel is structured around a cycle of lections.[5]

6. Luke wrote his Gospel approximately 90 c.e. for a Gentile Christian community, combining Mark and Matthew. He rewrote Matthew's birth narratives with the aid of the Hebrew Bible and freely elaborated Matthew.

7. John wrote approximately 100 c.e. for a community in Roman Asia, drawing on all three Synoptics (especially Matthew) and elaborating them freely.

8. The Gospel of Thomas is a gnosticizing version of the Synoptics (especially Luke) and contains no historical tradition or material pertinent to the understanding of the development of the Synoptics.

---

5. The lectionary theory of Matthew is presented in M. Goulder, *Midrash and Lection, the Evangelists' Calendar: A Lectionary Explanation of the Development of Scripture* (Speaker's Lectures in Biblical Studies 1972; London: SPCK, 1978); and idem, "Matthew's Gospel Round the Year," in this volume. This element of Goulder's thesis has attracted much criticism, since evidence of a fixed *siddur* of pentateuchal readings in the first century is highly ambiguous. See M. S. Goodacre, *Goulder and the Gospels: An Examination of a New Paradigm* (Journal for the Study of the New Testament Supplement 133; Sheffield: JSOT Press, 1996), 330–39: "Most of Goulder's evidence for the reading of the Pentateuch in an annual cycle beginning in Nisan is indirect and at best suggestive rather than probative" (339).

A few preliminary comments are in order. First, in terms of the logical architecture of his thesis, Goulder's fourth point (on Q) is actually a corollary of his sixth: if a case can be sustained for Luke's direct use of Matthew, there is no need to posit a non-Markan source in order to account for the double tradition material in Luke. Second, his seventh point (on John) is not directly relevant to a discussion of the Synoptic Problem, although his assessment of the relative amount of historical tradition in John depends on a convincing defense of the thesis of Johannine dependence on the Synoptics.[6] Third, the parallel issue of Thomas's relationship to the Synoptics is more crucial to Goulder's thesis, simply because of the extent of Synoptic-like material in Thomas. If Thomas were to contain sayings parallel to Matthew's non-Markan material — for example, Thomas's parable of the weeds (Gospel of Thomas 57) — that could not be shown to be dependent upon Matthew (hence, logically pre-Matthean), it would not be so simple for Goulder to account for the parable as a Matthean elaboration of Mark 4:26–29 (thus Goulder, MLM 367–69). Rather than offering his own analysis of the Thomas tradition, Goulder merely refers the reader to the works of Schrage and Ménard. This is unfortunate, since both are badly outdated and the case for independent tradition in Thomas is much stronger than I think Goulder suspects.[7] Independent tradition in Thomas might not overturn Goulder's thesis, but it would no doubt require added nuance.

The inferences that Goulder draws from his thesis are bold. First, he does away with pre-Gospel sources. The Q document disappears as a result of his theory of Lucan dependence on Matthew. Even more strikingly, Goulder's view of Matthew and Luke as creative, even inventive, editors of Mark (and, in the case of Luke, of Matthew) eliminates the need for special Matthean (M) or Lucan (L) sources. While it is true that few contemporary critics think M or L to be discrete documents, Goul-

---

6. The case for John's dependence on the Synoptics has found more defenders of late (e.g., F. Neirynck, "John and the Synoptics: 1975–1990," in *John and the Synoptics* [ed. A. Denaux; Bibliotheca ephemeridum theologicarum lovaniensium 101; Leuven: Peeters/Leuven University Press, 1992], 3–62), but is still far from *opinio communis*. See D. M. Smith, *John among the Gospels: The Relationship in Twentieth-Century Research* (Minneapolis: Fortress, 1992).

7. Goulder seems to have in mind W. Schrage's *Das Verhältnis des Thomas-Evangeliums zur synoptischen Tradition und zu den koptischen Evangelienübersetzungen* (Beihefte zur Zeitschrift für die neutestamentliche Wissenschaft 29; Berlin: Töpelmann, 1964) and J. E. Ménard's *L'évangile selon Thomas*

der does away with any need to appeal to pre-Matthean or pre-Lucan traditions. Thus Mark and Mark alone is the "beginning of the Gospel." Second and correspondingly, the degree of literary creativity in the later Gospels (and perhaps even in Mark) is very high. Not only is there no need for written documents such as Q, M, or L; there is little or nothing prior to or independent of Mark. Goulder's view of Luke's editorial procedure is consistent with the supposition of literary ingenuity, for he posits a Luke with extraordinary freedom in rewriting, manipulating, and rearranging his source material. One might observe that Goulder's thesis, if correct, would make reconstruction of the historical Jesus a rather simpler matter than is now usually imagined; or at least, he leaves us with fewer sources to worry about.

Goulder's thesis is articulated and defended with a combination of logic and brilliant rhetoric. It is perhaps this combination that accounts for the fact that in the United Kingdom at least, few scholars can take the 2DH as a given, and those who write on Q must at the same time be engaged in a defense of the 2DH; when they look over their shoulders, Goulder is always there.[8] Goulder has proved a formidable force in

---

(Nag Hammadi Studies 5; Leiden: Brill, 1975) (although he quotes neither) and refers to Schrage's thesis that the Coptic version of Thomas shows affinities with the Coptic versions of the New Testament. He fails, however, to note Schrage's later article, "Evangelienzitate in den Oxyrhynchus-Logien und im koptischen Thomas-Evangelium," in *Apophoreta: Festschrift für Ernst Haenchen zu seinem siebzigsten Geburtstag* (ed. W. Eltester and F. H. Kettler; Beihefte zur Zeitschrift für die neutestamentliche Wissenschaft 30; Berlin: Töpelmann, 1964), 251–68, which found the Oxyrhynchus fragments not to resemble the Greek New Testament as closely. This clearly opens the possibility of secondary assimilation of Coptic Thomas to the Coptic versions of the New Testament (or vice versa). For more recent discussions of the problem, see F. T. Fallon and R. Cameron, "The Gospel of Thomas: A Forschungsbericht and Analysis," in *Aufstieg und Niedergang der römischen Welt* 2.25.6 (1988): 4195–4251; C. W. Hedrick, "Thomas and the Synoptics: Aiming at a Consensus," *Second Century* 7 (1990): 39–56; C. M. Tuckett, "Das Thomasevangelium und die synoptischen Evangelien," *Berliner Theologische Zeitschrift* 12 (1995): 185–200; S. J. Patterson, "The Gospel of Thomas and the Synoptic Tradition: A Forschungsbericht and Critique," *Forum* 8 (1992): 45–97; idem, *The Gospel of Thomas and Jesus* (Foundations and Facets: Reference Series; Sonoma, Calif.: Polebridge, 1993). M. Fieger's comments on the issue in *Das Thomasevangelium: Einleitung, Kommentar und Systematik* (Neutestamentliche Abhandlungen 22; Münster: Aschendorff, 1991) are largely derivative of Schrage's older work.

8. Several important British studies of the Synoptic Problem defend the 2DH: C. M. Tuckett, *The Revival of the Griesbach Hypothesis: An Analysis and Appraisal* (Society for New Testament Studies Monograph 44; Cambridge: Cambridge University Press, 1983); M. D. Hooker, "The Son of Man and the Synoptic Problem," in *The Four Gospels 1992: Festschrift Frans Neirynck* (ed. F. Van Segbroeck, C. M. Tuckett, G. Van Belle, and J. Verheyden; Bibliotheca ephemeridum theologicarum lovaniensium 100; Leuven: Leuven University Press/Peeters, 1992), 189–201; P. M. Head, *Christology and the Synoptic Problem: An Assessment of One Argument for Markan Priority* (Society for New Testament Studies Monograph 94; Cambridge: Cambridge University Press, 1997). Q specialists in the United Kingdom are, in comparison with North America and Germany, relatively few: D. R. Catchpole, F. G. Downing,

the British New Testament establishment; and, though he complains of the lack of adherents his thesis has attracted, his influence is far from negligible.

Goulder calls his proposal a "new paradigm," expressly invoking a term popularized by Thomas Kuhn in *The Structure of Scientific Revolutions*.[9] In this critical reflection, I would like to ask three questions: What does Goulder mean by "paradigm"? Is Goulder's paradigm new? Does Goulder's thesis offer a compelling critique of the 2DH?

What Does Goulder Mean by "Paradigm"?

Ever since the publication of Kuhn's volume, the term *paradigm* has become rather a buzzword among theological writers. A quick consultation of the ATLA database shows that the word appears in the titles and abstracts of one thousand monographs and articles published since 1980, almost twelve hundred since 1970. Though a handful of these discuss the paradigms in the Greek and Hebrew verbal systems, many others expressly invoke Kuhn by announcing "shifting," "new," and "emerging" paradigms.

Some of these usages, no doubt, are rhetorical attempts to lend some unearned legitimacy to novel theses by claiming that they are part of "new" or "emerging" paradigms. The rhetorical appeal of the term is obvious. No one, after all, would wish to adhere to the old and dying view that combustion and rusting involves the release of phlogiston when Lavoisier's new paradigm of oxidation, reduction, and acidity is on the horizon. Nevertheless, it should be remembered that for Kuhn a paradigm is not merely an idea or a theory, but an achievement involving theories and practices (new ways of approaching the phenomena and new equipment) and promoting a new research program. The new research program in turn suggests new puzzles as well as solutions.[10] New

---

R. A. Piper, and C. M. Tuckett are the most prominent. C. L. Mearns and G. N. Stanton have also written on Q.

9. T. S. Kuhn, *The Structure of Scientific Revolutions* (2d ed.; International Encyclopedia of Unified Science, Foundations of the Unity of Science 2/2; Chicago: University of Chicago Press, 1970).

10. See C. Strug, "Kuhn's Paradigm Thesis: A Two-edged Sword for the Philosophy of Religion," *Religious Studies* 20 (1984): 269–79, esp. 270.

paradigms, moreover, are more easily recognized with hindsight than at the moment of their birth,[11] precisely because it takes some time for the paradigm to take hold in theory, in practices, and in the discursive modes adopted by practitioners.

Hence, advertisements of the birth of new paradigms (and the death of old ones) are always likely to be a bit premature. To be fair to Goulder, however, his rehabilitation of the Farrer theory, even if it has not attracted a significant group of practitioners, has been articulated over the course of twenty-five years and has achieved a practical embodiment in two significant commentaries, one on Matthew and another on Luke. It is not clear to me, nevertheless, that Goulder's theory has done what Kuhnian paradigms ought to do, namely, to suggest a new set of problems to be solved. And as I shall suggest below, Goulder's theory involves no substantially new practices or tools: Goulder remains a redaction critic, and a fine one at that, employing the standard tools of the trade in a relatively conventional manner.

Falsifiability: Goulder's Popperian View

In order to probe more deeply into what Goulder means by paradigm, it is useful to examine the opening paragraphs of *Luke: A New Paradigm*. There he refers to both Karl Popper[12] and Kuhn, arguing (with Popper) that knowledge progresses by conjectures, which are then subjected to deductive testing that attempts to refute them. For Popper, conjectures that survive are not thereby shown to be certainly true or even as probably correct, but they do appear to us to be better approximations of the truth than competing conjectures which fail deductive testing.[13] Falsifiability — the susceptibility of a hypothesis to refutation by means of empirical observations — is for Popper what sets scientific conjectures apart from nonscientific ones.[14]

---

11. As Kuhn notes, it is sometimes even difficult to identify the point at which a paradigm-shifting discovery occurs, as in the case of the discovery of oxygen in the 1770s. See *Structure of Scientific Revolutions*, 53–56.

12. K. Popper, *The Logic of Scientific Discovery* (London: Hutchinson, 1959 [first English ed.], 1968 [rev. ed.]); idem, *Conjectures and Refutations: The Growth of Scientific Knowledge* (London: Routledge & Kegan Paul, 1963).

13. Popper, *Conjectures and Refutations*, vii; idem, *Logic of Scientific Discovery*, 32–33.

14. This is Popper's criterion of demarcation between scientific and nonscientific (and metaphysical) statements: "I proposed that *refutability or falsifiability* of a theoretical system should be taken as

Goulder describes the 2DH as a paradigm or "complex of hypothe-ses" that includes a conjectured sayings source Q and the hypothesis of the independence of Matthew and Luke. Since on most accounts Q's contents did not include material parallel to the Markan passion narrative,[15] the 2DH implies that, while in Mark 1–13 there might be Matthew-Luke agreements against Mark that result from their incorpo-ration of Q into the Markan framework, there should be no significant agreements of Matthew and Luke against Mark in the passion narrative. This is a simple deductive test, and one which, apparently, the 2DH fails: there is at least one significant minor agreement, Matt 26:67–68 || Luke 22:63–64 against Mark 14:65 (see n. 35 below).

I will return to the issue of the minor agreements later, but for the moment it is important to observe that Goulder's understanding of a paradigm corresponds to Popper's idea of the "problem situation" or "framework" into which the scientist fits her own work.[16] For Popper, it is a truism that the scientist works within a definite theoretical framework; but he emphasizes that "at any moment" the scientist can challenge and break out of that framework.[17] Popper in fact rejects Kuhn's model of a single dominant, controlling paradigm. On the contrary, multiple competing theories exist at any given time; they are generally commensu-rable; and, if scientific, they are falsifiable. For Popper, science progresses in a continuous process of conjectures and refutations, with multiple conjectures vying for dominance.

This erodes Kuhn's distinction between normal and extraordinary sci-

---

the criterion of demarcation. According to this view, which I still uphold, a system is to be considered as scientific only if it makes assertions which may clash with observations; and a system is, in fact, tested by attempts to produce such clashes, that is to say by attempts to refute it. Thus testability is the same as refutability, and can therefore likewise be taken as a criterion of demarcation" (*Conjectures and Refutations*, 256; emphasis original).

15. Goulder's statement is much stronger: "Now Q is *defined* as a body of sayings material and some narrative, beginning from the preaching of John and ending before the Passion" (*LNP* 6 [emphasis added]); and "there is no Q in the Passion story *ex hypothesi*." This misleadingly makes it seem that the definition of Q is stipulative and, correspondingly, makes its refutation analytic (based on a simple understanding of the meaning of terms) rather than *a posteriori*. In fact, Q is only "defined" as the non-Markan source of Matthew and Luke. It *turns out* not to have passion sayings, but this is not part of the definition of Q.

16. K. Popper, "Normal Science and Its Dangers," in *Criticism and the Growth of Knowledge* (ed. I. Lakatos and A. Musgrave; Proceedings of the International Colloquium in the Philosophy of Science 4; Cambridge: Cambridge University Press, 1970), 51–58, esp. 51.

17. Ibid., 56.

ence, between those phases of scientific research generally informed on the one hand by one broad conceptual paradigm, related practices, and commending a certain research program and on the other hand by transitional periods when a prevailing paradigm has become problematized due to a critical mass of uncooperative data and anomalous observations, which eventually lead to its displacement by a new paradigm. Indeed Popper understands Kuhn's term *normal science* in a pejorative sense, connoting the activity of the "nonrevolutionary" and "not-too-critical professional," "the science student who accepts the ruling dogma of the day."[18]

Paradigm, for Goulder, has a Popperian ring, despite the fact that the subtitle of his Luke book advertises a new paradigm. To be sure, Goulder takes from Kuhn the idea that dominant paradigms often accommodate anomalies by making ad hoc adjustments. But while Kuhn takes such adaptations to be a standard and necessary part of normal science,[19] Goulder sees the attempts of the 2DH to accommodate anomalies by adjusting the theory — positing other intermediate documents, or oral tradition, or textual corruption — as leading to an "elastic," unfalsifiable, and therefore unscientific hypothesis. He observes, moreover, that paradigms resist displacement because researchers have invested careers in research programs informed by those paradigms. For Goulder, as for

18. Ibid., 52. Similarly, *Logic of Scientific Discovery*, 50: "A system such as classical mechanics may be 'scientific' to any degree you like; but those who uphold it dogmatically — believing, perhaps, that it is their business to defend such a successful system against criticism as long as it is not *conclusively disproved* — are adopting the very reverse of that critical attitude which in my view is the proper one for the scientist. In point of fact, no conclusive disproof of a theory can ever be produced; for it is always possible to say that the experimental results are not reliable, or that the discrepancies which are asserted to exist between the experimental results and the theory are only apparent and that they will disappear with the advance of our understanding. If you insist on strict proof (or strict disproof) in the empirical sciences, you will never benefit from experience, and never learn from it how wrong you are."

19. T. S. Kuhn, "Logic of Discovery or Psychology of Research?" in *Criticism and the Growth of Knowledge* (ed. I. Lakatos and A. Musgrave; Proceedings of the International Colloquium in the Philosophy of Science 4; Cambridge: Cambridge University Press, 1970), 1–23, esp. 13: "It is important, furthermore, that this should be so, for it is often by challenging observations or adjusting theories that scientific knowledge grows. Challenges and adjustments are a standard part of normal research in empirical science, and adjustments, at least, play a dominant role in informal mathematics as well." Contrast Popper's statement in *Logic of Scientific Discovery*, 42: "For it is always possible to find some way of evading falsification, for example by introducing *ad hoc* an auxiliary hypothesis, or by changing *ad hoc* a definition. It is even possible without logical inconsistency to adopt the position of simply refusing to acknowledge any falsifying experience whatsoever. Admittedly, scientists do not usually proceed in this way, but logically such procedure is possible; and this fact, it might be claimed, makes the logical value of my proposed criterion of demarcation dubious, to say the least."

Popper, paradigms ought to be susceptible to deductive testing, which could well lead to their immediate collapse. The fact that they do not collapse is a symptom of the dangers of normal science.[20] Thus he bemoans the fact that generations of graduate students internalize and then perpetuate a paradigm which, he thinks, is logically flawed ("Juggernaut," 668). Throughout his introduction to *Luke: A New Paradigm,* he refers to adherents of the 2DH with the apparently pejorative term *paradigmers.*

Kuhn's reply to Popper is that paradigms, precisely because of their complexity, can seldom be cast in a form that is susceptible to the sort of deductive refutation that Popper (or Goulder) seeks. Tolerance of anomalies is not a special characteristic of paradigms that are about to collapse or of paradigms that irrationally resist falsification — it is a mark of all paradigms. For example, Schrödinger wave mechanics and his wave equation produce coherent results with electrons traveling much below the speed of light; but at higher velocities, and for other particles traveling near light-speed, Schrödinger's equation does not work. The equation produces coherent results for electrons in the hydrogen atom, but not for atoms that have a more complex constellation of electrons and orbitals. But this is not a reason to abandon the Schrödinger wave equation. Nor does the fact that light and other electromagnetic radiation exhibit some of the features of particles (e.g., mass equivalence and momentum) imply that the wave theory of light is unusable. The wave theory continues to account for much observable data and serves as the basis for the construction of optical theory.

It is for reasons such as these that paradigms in Kuhn's sense do not collapse when faced with bits of anomalous data. An old paradigm is declared invalid only when anomalies have accumulated to the extent

---

20. Popper, "Normal Science," 52–53. Goulder (*LNP* 4) asserts that Kuhn's use of "normal science" is pejorative, but this seems to be a case of reading Kuhn via Popper. Kuhn (*Structure of Scientific Revolutions,* 65) in fact sees normal science not as antithetical to extraordinary science, but as embodying the practices that lead to its own displacement: "By ensuring that the paradigm will not be too easily surrendered, resistance guarantees that scientists will not be lightly distracted and that the anomalies that lead to paradigm change will penetrate existing knowledge to the core. The very fact that a significant scientific novelty so often emerges simultaneously from several laboratories is an index both to the strongly traditional nature of normal science and to the completeness with which that traditional pursuit prepares the way for its own change."

that the paradigm cannot bear their weight and when a new candidate emerges to take its place. The choice to abandon one is simultaneously a choice to embrace another.[21]

Goulder's Popperian perspective on the issue of the falsification of scientific hypotheses and his Popperian sense of paradigms helps to account for the strategy he adopts in criticizing the 2DH: he proposes simple deductive tests — principally, the presence of minor agreements and the presence of Matthean vocabulary in Luke — with the expectation that such tests should refute the theory, leaving place for his own. This is also why he prefers as dialogue partners the so-called hardliners Neirynck and Tuckett, who respond to the issue of the minor agreements by suggesting either coincidental redaction by Matthew and Luke or textual corruption.[22] This is in contrast to soft-liners, who appeal to multiple recensions of Mark, the interference of oral tradition, or intermediate Gospels. The hard-line position, because it requires its exponents to be able to supply plausible redaction-critical reasons for a coincidental agreement in altering Mark or to point to an early and reliable manuscript that eliminates the minor agreement, is, Goulder believes, easily falsifiable. This argumentative strategy can be seen not only in *Luke: A New Paradigm* but also in many of Goulder's articles and essays. Thus, while he invokes Kuhn, the key issue for Goulder is Popperian falsification. The existence of a paradigm accounts only for the resistance encountered by new proposals. It is a term connoting institutional inertia.[23]

I wish to suggest two reasons why Goulder's criticism of the 2DH has not proved effective and his own theory has not been embraced — a fact conceded by Goulder himself. First is that Goulder's Popperian view

---

21. Kuhn, *Structure of Scientific Revolutions*, 77.

22. On the notorious minor agreement at Mark 14:65, see C. M. Tuckett, "On the Relationship between Matthew and Luke," *New Testament Studies* 30 (1984): 130–42; and F. Neirynck, "Τίς ἐστιν ὁ παίσας σε: Mt 26,68/Lk 22,64 (diff. Mk 14,65)," *Ephemerides theologicae lovanienses* 63 (1987): 5–47; repr. with an additional note in *Evangelica II: 1982–1991 Collected Essays* (ed. F. Van Segbroeck; Bibliotheca ephemeridum theologicarum lovaniensium 99; Leuven: Leuven University Press, 1991), 94–138.

23. Goulder ("Juggernaut," 668–69) ventures that modern support for the 2DH is due to a combination of inertia, personal attachments, lack of academic integrity in admitting "that [proponents] have been wrong for years" and the daunting mass of scholarly literature on the topic that few can read or master. Missing from Goulder's list is the possibility that some embrace the 2DH on the basis of a careful examination of Synoptic data and the explanations that best account for those data.

of falsification is not shared by most of those he criticizes. The 2DH is believed to be able to accommodate anomalies, just as Kuhn's paradigms routinely both produce and accommodate anomalies in the course of the puzzle solving of normal science. The 2DH is not perceived as imperiled by the problem of the minor agreements, and it provides a generally coherent account of a host of Synoptic data. Simply put, the 2DH is still an effective hypothesis. The second reason is that Goulder's thesis produces its own puzzles having to do with Luke's editorial procedures that Goulder has not sufficiently addressed. I will return to some of these later, but for the moment I would like to comment on falsification and the 2DH.

Are Synoptic Theories Falsifiable?

When it was first formulated, the 2DH — or at least the supposition of (Ur-)Markan priority and the existence of sayings source — was advertised as incorrigible, beyond falsification. Albert Schweitzer, Holtzmann's erstwhile student at Strasbourg, is a good example of such rhetorical bravado: "The [Markan] hypothesis has a literary existence, indeed it is carried out by Holtzmann to such a degree of demonstration that it can no longer be called a mere hypothesis."[24] A half century later Willi Marxsen echoed this:

> This Two-Sources theory has been so widely accepted by scholars that one feels inclined to abandon the term "theory" (in the sense of "hypothesis"). We can in fact regard it as an assured finding — but we must bear in mind that there are inevitable uncertainties as far as the extent and form of Q and the special material are concerned.[25]

---

24. A. Schweitzer, *The Quest of the Historical Jesus* (preface by F. C. Burkitt; New York: Macmillan, 1910; repr. 1968), 202.

25. W. Marxsen, *Introduction to the New Testament: An Approach to Its Problems* (Philadelphia: Fortress, 1968), 118. Similarly, W. G. Kümmel (*Introduction to the New Testament* [rev. ed.; Nashville: Abingdon, 1975], 64) asserts that Luke's direct dependence on Matthew was "completely inconceivable" (*völlig undenkbar*), but acknowledges the existence of proponents of just this view: K. H. Rengstorff, A. Schlatter, J. H. Ropes, B. C. Butler, A. M. Farrer, N. Turner, W. R. Farmer, A. W. Argyle, R. T. Simpson, W. Wilkens, and E. P. Sanders.

This is a grave logical mistake that has now been exposed, thanks in part to the efforts of John Chapman, B. C. Butler, W. R. Farmer, and Michael Goulder himself. Happily, it is difficult to find such inflated rhetorical claims made by contemporary adherents of the 2DH. The 2DH is and remains a hypothesis. Deductive testing might refute a hypothesis, but it can never prove one or establish it as fact.

Ironically, perhaps, proponents of other hypotheses have sometimes succumbed to the temptation of similar rhetoric. For example, in the defense of the 2GH offered by McNicol and his colleagues, McNicol repeatedly describes data in Luke (either the sequence of Lucan materials or certain phrases or words) as "evidence" of Luke's direct use of Matthew.[26] It is not evidence or proof; rather, it is data for which the 2GH may offer a plausible accounting, but for which the 2GH is not the only plausible accounting. A yet more blatant example of rhetorical overstatement comes from Goulder's mentor, Austin Farrer:

> The Q hypothesis is a hypothesis, that is its weakness. To be rid of it we have no need of a contrary hypothesis, we merely have to make St. Luke's use of St. Matthew intelligible; and to understand what St. Luke made of St. Matthew we need no more than to consider what St. Luke made of his own book. Now St. Luke's book is not a hypothetical entity. Here is a copy of it on my desk.[27]

This is a sleight of hand. Luke indeed "existed" on Farrer's desk, though Farrer did not seem to notice that the Greek text which he had on his desk was itself the *reconstruction* of text critics such as Tischendorff, Westcott, Hort, and Nestle who depended upon *hypotheses* concerning the transmission of the text of Luke. What did not exist on Farrer's desk, however, was Luke's *relationship* to Matthew. That was Farrer's hypothesis, and that is his "weakness."

---

26. McNicol, Dungan, and Peabody, *Beyond the Q Impasse,* 18 (sequential parallels between Luke 3:1–10:22, divided into five sections, and the sequence of Matt 3:1–18:5), 23 (agreements of Luke 4:31–32; 7:1 with Matt 7:28–29), 24 (Luke's use of the Matthean absolute genitive + *idou*, Luke's use of a participial form of *proserchomai* to introduce a finite verb [23:52], and Luke's use of *skandalizein*). In the summary (318–19), McNicol claims that this data can be explained *only* on the 2GH, even though other explanations are not entertained.

27. Farrer, "On Dispensing with Q"; repr. 321–56, esp. 333.

Goulder engages in similar rhetorical flourishes when he asserts: "Luke's use of Mark is a fact (or generally accepted as one), while Q is a mere postulate"; and further, "Q is now hardly defended in the University of Oxford."[28] Goulder's subordinate clause, "Q is a mere postulate," is perfectly correct: Q is a postulate of the hypothesis that affirms both the priority of Mark to Matthew and Luke and the mutual independence of Matthew and Luke. One may quibble only with Goulder's adjective *mere*. Q is not a "mere" postulate; on the contrary, it follows *necessarily* from the two logically prior postulates.[29]

As to Luke's use of Mark being a "fact" or even a "generally accepted fact," neither is the case. The key piece of data from the Synoptic Gospels — that Matthew and Luke never agree against Mark in the sequence of triple tradition pericopes[30] — admits (logically speaking) of any explanation that places Mark in a medial position. This includes the 2DH and the Farrer-Goulder hypothesis (FGH). This datum, however, is also explicable, for example, on the 2GH and Boismard's multistage hypothesis, which allows only a mediated relationship between Mark and Luke.[31] Such explanations are hypotheses, not unassailable facts. Moreover, whether Luke used Mark (2DH, FGH) or Mark used Luke (2GH) or both derived from some intermediary (Boismard) cannot conclusively be proved or disproved, since virtually all of the directional indicators are stylistic or theological, and most or all of the arguments are reversible. Luke's use of Mark thus remains a hypothesis — a reasonable and effec-

---

28. Goulder, "Juggernaut," 670, 668. The irony of the latter statement is that by the time that this article appeared, C. M. Tuckett, one of the ablest defenders of the 2DH, had come to Oxford.

29. Similarly, C. M. Tuckett, "The Existence of Q," in *The Gospel behind the Gospels: Current Studies on Q* (ed. R. A. Piper; Novum Testamentum Supplement 75; Leiden: Brill, 1995), 21 = Q *and the History of Early Christianity: Studies on Q* (Edinburgh: T&T Clark; Peabody, Mass.: Hendrickson, 1996), 4, who rightly calls the Q hypothesis a "negative theory" insofar as it is predicated on the denial of a direct relationship between Matthew and Luke. Because Q is an integral part of the 2DH, it is infelicitous to speak of the Q hypothesis as if it were logically separable from the 2DH.

30. See E. P. Sanders, "The Argument from Order and the Relationship between Matthew and Luke," *New Testament Studies* 15 (1968–69): 249–61; and the answers by F. Neirynck, "The Argument from Order and St. Luke's Transpositions," *Ephemerides theologicae lovanienses* 49 (1973): 784–815; and R. H. Fuller, "Order in the Synoptic Gospels: A Summary," *Second Century* 6 (1987–88): 107–9.

31. This is characteristic of all of Boismard's slightly varying solutions. In *Evangile de Marc: Sa préhistoire* (Études bibliques n.s. 26; Paris: Cerf, 1994), Luke and Matthew are dependent on an intermediate version of Mark (Mark[int]), and the final version of Mark is dependent on a Marco-Lucan editor. His 1972 hypothesis lacked Mark's dependence on a "rédacteur marco-lucanien" but affirmed the dependence of Mark and Luke on Mark[int]. See M.-E. Boismard, *Synopse des quatre évangiles en français*, vol. 2: *Commentaire* (preface by P. Benoit; Paris: Cerf, 1972).

tive hypothesis, in my view — but no volume of scholarly literature in its support (and no voting from Oxford — or Toronto, for that matter) will elevate its ontological status to anything more than that.

The Nature of Synoptic Hypotheses

If we set aside the various rhetorical overstatements, we are still left with the broader conceptual question of the nature and function of competing Synoptic hypotheses. It is foolish to claim incorrigibility, but equally mistaken to insist on the degree of simplicity that Goulder's requirement of falsifiability implies. In the formulation of hypotheses concerning the Synoptic Gospels, we are caught between two incompatible constraints: on the one hand, to formulate hypotheses that are as simple and clear as possible and that are generally falsifiable by reference to the array of Synoptic data; and on the other, to formulate hypotheses that are sufficiently attentive to the complexity of technological and human factors involved in the production and transmission of the Gospels to be a near approximation to what might have happened. Moreover, Synoptic hypotheses are not pictures or reconstructions of "what happened." They are only heuristic tools that offer convenient lenses through which to view data.

From the point of view of logic, it clearly is desirable to have a simple theory according to which Matthew and Luke used Mark — a supposition common to both the FGH and the 2DH. It is, however, most improbable from a historical perspective that Matthew and Luke used the same copy of Mark. Given what we know about the early transmission of manuscripts, it is highly unlikely that any two copies of Mark were in every respect identical. After all, none of the early papyri of the Gospels is identical with another. Two copies of Mark would at a minimum be subject to copyists' mistakes and conceivably to more substantial alterations. There is, moreover, no reason to suppose that Matthew's Mark and our Mark are identical, or that Luke's Mark was identical with either. The same considerations apply, *mutatis mutandis*, to Q on the 2DH or to Matthew and Luke on the 2GH.[32]

---

32. This assertion might appear odd, coming from one of the three editors of *Documenta Q* and the critical edition of Q by the International Q Project. I do not, however, believe that in text-critical

Synoptic hypotheses are convenient simplifications of what was undoubtedly a much more complex, and unrecoverable, process of composition and transmission. Under such circumstances, it seems perverse to insist on simple pictures that we know in advance to be too simple, merely because they are also easily falsifiable, or to bemoan the resort to more ornate solutions on the grounds that certain features of the more ornate hypotheses place them beyond falsification.

The Minor Agreements and the Two Document Hypothesis

The agreement of Matthew and Luke against Mark is the key problem for the 2DH. Some proponents of the 2DH accommodate the minor agreements by adjusting the model of the 2DH, suggesting recensions of Mark (Ur-Markus or Deutero-Markus) which agreed with Matthew and Luke; others account for the minor agreements by the supposition of interference from oral tradition; still others suggest textual (post-Markan) corruption; and a few posit intermediate Gospels. Goulder objects to most of these strategies since they place the hypothesis beyond falsification.

While Goulder's point is well taken, it is also the case that none of the adjustments mentioned above is inherently implausible. First, other literature existed in multiple recensions: the Greek and Coptic versions of the Gospel of Thomas, for example, display significant variations, including abbreviation and contractions of sayings and the relocation of one saying to a new context.[33] Second, as recent studies of ancient literacy show, oral performance was involved in literary production at several stages. Composition sometimes involved preliminary drafts, oral recitation before select audiences, and final editing taking into account the audience reaction. Moreover, the difficulties inherent in reading texts written *scripta continua* meant that in the performance/reading of a work,

---

labors or in the reconstructive efforts of the International Q Project it is realistic or theoretically possible to reconstruct *the* original text of a Gospel or Q. What is reconstructed is an imaginary point on a complex continuum of textual production and textual transmission. This imaginary point presumably approximates to a near degree a document that once existed; but its primary theoretical function is to account for preceding and subsequent textual history, to the extent that this is known.

33. Compare the abbreviation of Oxyrhynchus papyrus 655.1.1–17 in Gospel of Thomas 36 and the expansion of Oxyrhynchus papyrus 654.5–9 in Gospel of Thomas 2. The second part of Oxyrhynchus papyrus 1.22–30 (= Gospel of Thomas 30) is found in Coptic as Gospel of Thomas 77.

the text functioned in a manner to a musical score rather than a document to be recited.[34] This means that the way a work was heard was a combination of textual and (oral) performative features, or to put it differently, when we read ancient texts, we see only part of what was actually heard. Finally, the study of early New Testament papyri shows a remarkably unstable textual situation, with harmonization and parallel influence attested at a very early stage. If such variation is empirically attested in early New Testament manuscripts, it seems perverse to insist on a scenario that forecloses the possibility of transcriptional variations between multiple copies of Mark and Q.

Given these facts, it makes no sense to insist, as Goulder does, on mathematically simple hypotheses. The imperative of Synoptic Problem research is not to produce generalizations or schematic models simply so that they achieve a state of maximal falsifiability; the task of research is to produce models that account for as much of the data as possible. Any one of the adjustments to the 2DH noted above is capable of accommodating the few significant minor agreements — and they are relatively few.[35] If there is a difficulty with the 2DH, it is not that it cannot give an account of the minor agreements; rather, it is that we do not know which of the several available adjustments is preferable.

This view is bound not to please Goulder, but it is a realistic approach

---

34. K. Quinn, "The Poet and His Audience in the Augustan Age," *Aufstieg und Niedergang der römischen Welt* 2.30.1 (1982): 75–180, esp. 90.

35. Although a raw tabulation of the minor agreements produces seemingly impressive numbers — 610 positive and 573 negative agreements by Ennulat's counting — many of these are "agreements" only in the most general sense and hardly imply any collaboration of Matthew and Luke; others are rather easily explained on the basis of Matthean and Lucan redactional habits. There are a small number of difficult cases:

Matt 13:11 || Luke 8:10 against Mark 4:11
Matt 9:20 || Luke 8:44 (*tou kraspedou*) against Mark 5:27
Matt 9:26 || Luke 4:14 (not in the same Markan context)
Matt 22:34–40 || Luke 10:25–28 (which some ascribe to Q) against Mark 12:12–34
Matt 26:67–68 || Luke 22:63–64 against Mark 14:65
Matt 26:75 || Luke 22:62 against Mark 14:72
Matt 28:1 || Luke 23:54 (*epiphōskein*) against Mark 16:1

See A. Ennulat, *Die "Minor Agreements": Untersuchung zu einer offenen Frage des synoptischen Problems* (Wissenschaftliche Untersuchungen zum Neuen Testament 2/62; Tübingen: Mohr [Siebeck], 1994); and my review in *Toronto Journal of Theology* 13 (1997): 101–3. The fundamental work on the minor agreements is still F. Neirynck, *The Minor Agreements of Matthew and Luke against Mark: With a Cumulative List* (Bibliotheca ephemeridum theologicarum lovaniensium 37; Leuven: Leuven University Press, 1974).

under the circumstances. It does render falsification of the 2DH more difficult but not, I think, impossible. The 2DH allows for a coherent accounting of both Matthew's and Luke's editorial practices and although it also generates some anomalies, these are no more serious than those generated on other hypotheses.

Is Goulder's "Paradigm" New?

There is little doubt about the novelty of Goulder's theory of Synoptic relationships. While there are some anticipations in the nineteenth century in the work of Karl Credner and closer comrades in J. H. Ropes and Morton Enslin,[36] Goulder's theory is far more learned and ambitious than those of his predecessors, for he accounts for most of the non-Markan material in Matthew and Luke as the result of redactional invention by the evangelists.

The Kuhnian question, however, is, "Is this a new paradigm?" The answer is, I think, "no." A paradigm for Kuhn is significantly larger than a particular theory or hypothesis. A paradigm both "stands for the entire constellation of beliefs, values, techniques, and so on, shared by the members of a given [research] community"; and it is "the concrete puzzle-solutions which, employed as models or examples, can replace explicit rules as a basis for the solution of the remaining puzzles of normal science."[37] Moreover, as Margaret Masterman observes, in the genealogy of a new paradigm it is often not the formal theory that comes first, but what she calls a "trick, or an embryonic technique, or picture, and an insight that is applicable to the field."[38] This combination of trick and

---

36. K. A. Credner, *Einleitung in das Neue Testament* (Halle: Waisenhauses, 1836), 201–5, who (a) posited Luke's dependence on Matthew and both on an Aramaic proto-Gospel also used by Mark and (b) invoked the *Logia* source to account for the double tradition; J. H. Ropes, *The Synoptic Gospels* (Cambridge: Harvard University Press; London: Oxford University Press, 1934; with new preface: London: Oxford University Press, 1960), 66–68, 93–94; M. Enslin, *Christian Beginnings* (New York, Harper, 1938), 431–34.

37. Kuhn, "Postscript — 1969," in *Structure of Scientific Revolutions*, 175. Kuhn calls the first sense "sociological" and the second sense a "shared example." M. Masterman ("The Nature of a Paradigm," in *Criticism and the Growth of Knowledge* [ed. I. Lakatos and A. Musgrave; Proceedings of the International Colloquium in the Philosophy of Science 4; Cambridge: Cambridge University Press, 1970], 59–89, esp. 67) refers to the second as a construct paradigm.

38. Masterman, "Nature of a Paradigm," 69.

insight constitutes the paradigm, which is then worked out in explicit theory and more advanced techniques.

As an example, one might think of advances in quantum mechanics. Faced with Compton's evidence that X-rays had particle as well as wave properties, de Broglie suggested that all matter has both particle and wave properties. De Broglie's hunch was tested with defraction devices, which had been employed ever since Augustin-Jean Fresnel's 1815 experiments that had demonstrated wave theory in visible light. Instead of defracting electromagnetic radiation, Davisson and Germer tried electrons and showed in 1927 that they too could be defracted and hence exhibited wave properties. Only later did Schrödinger's wave mechanics provide the mathematical resolution of the two seemingly opposed characteristics of electrons.

The main paradigm shift in the study of the Gospels came, not with Goulder or even Holtzmann, but in the late eighteenth century, with Reimarus and Griesbach. Since the time of Tatian, Celsus, and Porphyry, the disagreements among the Gospels were well known, but were resolved in two different manners. Augustine, in his *De consensu evangelistarum,* treated differences among the Gospels as divergent yet ultimately compatible depictions of Christ: Matthew focusing on royalty, Mark on humanity, Luke on priesthood, and John on divinity. The differences among the Gospels could not gainsay the truth of the gospel, the latter understood in Augustine's Platonism as a transcendental idea that was partially and perspectively embodied in the text of the Gospels.[39] A different strategy was employed by harmonists, who referred disagreements to the artificially constructed metatext of the Gospel harmony. This practice came under increasing pressure with the advent, in the sixteenth century, of a verbally based doctrine of inspiration. Andreas Osiander's *Harmonia evangelica* insisted that even small variations in seemingly parallel accounts were significant and indicated discrete

---

39. S. McLoughlin notices Augustine's Platonism in "An Approach to the Synoptic Problem" (S.T.L. thesis, Katholieke Universiteit Leuven, 1963): "Augustine speaks of Mk following Mt, and while in our scientifically-minded age such a suggestion carries causal implications, it is much less certain that it does so for the Platonic-minded Augustine: a second witness, who adds nothing to what the first and principal witness had already said, could well in such a mentality be described as his follower" (28).

historical events.[40] Thus he desynchronized pericopes that earlier harmonists had treated as parallel, a policy that produced in his synopsis, and those that followed him, a string of absurd repetitions. Osiander, for example, had three healings of blind men near Jericho, three centurions' sons healed, three anointings of Jesus, and three cleansings of the temple.[41]

A new paradigm emerged with an insight concerning the "particularity" or individuality of each Gospel. Particularity had been a feature of Osiander's harmony insofar as particularities of the Gospels were registered as discrete events in his metatext. But particularity took on a new significance when Hermann Samuel Reimarus argued that the contradictions among the Gospels implied that their authors had produced inconsistent, indeed fraudulent, accounts of Jesus' career.[42] For Reimarus the Gospels were discrete works, not related to some reconciling metatext. Instead, he viewed the Gospels in relation to a plausible historical reconstruction of their referent (Jesus) and their composers (the evangelists).

This turn toward the particularity of the Gospels was made possible by a new "device," the three-Gospel synopsis, created by J. J. Griesbach at virtually the same moment.[43] Griesbach's synopsis allowed for the first time a close comparison of agreements and disagreements among the Gospels. In retrospect, one might locate a paradigm shift in Griesbach's stated refusal to embrace the harmonist's program of creating a harmonious narrative, for this was impossible in principle.[44]

The "trick" of the new paradigm of Gospel study is Synoptic compar-

---

40. A. Osiander, *Harmoniae evangelicae libri quatuor Graece et Latine* (Geneva: Stephani, 1537).

41. See the discussion of pre-Griesbach synopses in H. K. McArthur, *The Quest through the Centuries: The Search for the Historical Jesus* (Philadelphia: Fortress, 1966), 85–101; and M. H. de Lang, "Gospel Synopses from the 16th to the 18th Centuries and the Rise of Literary Criticism of the Gospels," in *The Synoptic Gospels: Source Criticism and New Literary Criticism* (ed. C. Focant; Bibliotheca ephemeridum theologicarum lovaniensium 110; Leuven: Leuven University Press/Peeters, 1993), 599–607.

42. H. S. Reimarus, "Von dem Zwecke Jesu und seiner Jünger," in *Fragmente des Wolfenbüttelschen Ungenannten* (ed. G. Lessing; Berlin: Sanders [Eichhoff], 1778) = *Fragments* (ed. C. H. Talbert; trans. R. S. Fraser; Philadelphia: Fortress, 1970).

43. The synopsis originally appeared in 1774 as part of Griesbach's *Libri historici Novi Testamenti graece* (Halle: Curtius, 1774) and was printed separately two years later as *Synopsis Evangeliorum Matthaei, Marc et Lucae* (Halle: Curtius, 1776).

44. J. J. Griesbach, *Synopsis Evangeliorum Matthaei, Marci et Lucae, una cum iis Joannis pericopis; Quae historiam passionis et resurrectionis Jesu Christi complectuntur* (2d ed.; Halle: Curtius, 1797), v–vi.

ison, made possible first by the critical synopsis and subsequently by the many tabular comparisons of the sequence of Synoptic pericopes and the special and shared vocabulary of the Gospels, culminating in sophisticated tools such as Morgenthaler's *Statistische Synopse,* Neirynck's *New Testament Vocabulary,* and the Hoffmann-Hieke-Bauer *Synoptic Concordance.*[45]

The combination of an insight (the historical particularity of the Gospels) and a device (the synopsis) constituted a paradigm in which the puzzle-solving of normal science could take place. This took the form of a succession of attempts to solve the literary puzzle of the relationship of the Synoptics, first in the rather loose and impressionistic theories of Lessing and Herder, then in the baroque source theories of Eichhorn, then in Saunier and de Wette's popularization of the Griesbach hypothesis, and finally in Holtzmann's rehabilitation of C. H. Weisse's 1938 Two-Source theory. What is common to these theories and to the Streeterian Four-Source hypothesis, the FGH, and the 2GH which followed them is that, as divergent as they may seem, they no longer refer differences to some metanarrative, but understand differences to be the function of the literary, historical, and rhetorical particularity.

In the course of two centuries of Gospel study many variations of the paradigm have been introduced. Source criticism in the nineteenth century seemed to prefer a rather strict documentary approach, not entertaining the possibility of the influence of oral tradition upon the writers. This habit accounts both for the positing of intermediate documents such as Ur-Markus to account for slight differences between canonical Mark and the "Mark" which Matthew and Luke seemed to use and for the scouring of patristic sources for references to possibly important lost documents such as the Gospel of the Hebrews or Papias's *Logia.* In the early twentieth century, appeal to the interference of oral tradition became a standard part of many Synoptic theories; and by mid-century, the advent of redaction criticism obviated the theoretical need

---

45. R. Morgenthaler, *Statistische Synopse* (Zürich and Stuttgart: Gotthelf, 1971); F. Neirynck and F. Van Segbroeck, *New Testament Vocabulary: A Companion Volume to the Concordance* (Bibliotheca ephemeridum theologicarum lovaniensium 65; Leuven: Peeters/Leuven University Press, 1984); P. Hoffmann, T. Hieke, and U. Bauer, *Synoptic Concordance: A Greek Concordance to the First Three Gospels in Synoptic Arrangement, Statistically Evaluated* (4 vols.; Berlin: de Gruyter, 1999–).

to posit earlier forms of Mark or Matthew, since differences, including additions, deletions, and modifications, could plausibly be referred to the creativity of the evangelists.

In this sense, Goulder's theory is a utilization hypothesis that accounts for the differences between Matthew and Mark and between Luke and Matthew/Mark by appealing to a now-standard lexicon of editorial maneuvers: abbreviation, expansion, transposition, rewriting, and free invention. All of this fits snugly within the prevailing paradigm of Synoptic research, despite its nonconformity with the 2DH, the dominant source theory (not paradigm) of Synoptic relationships.

Genuinely new paradigms might be on the horizon — one thinks of the narrative approaches, which often prescind from diachronic features of composition and focus on the narrative syntax of the Gospel text. There may even be a new device, the Gospel parallel, which allows each Gospel to be viewed in its narrative integrity rather than cutting the text into source-critical or form-critical slices.[46] Or again, the turn toward social history has discovered the tool of the Mediterranean anthropologist's field report and has applied some of her conceptual categories to the Gospel text. Whether such innovations will turn out to offer a new paradigm may be doubted, however; both synchronic aspects of the Gospel text and the constellation of embedded social values have now been subsumed in socio-rhetorical exegesis.[47] In any event, neither narrative approaches nor social-scientific approaches have served to solve the puzzles endemic to the study of the Synoptic Problem.

Is the Two Document Hypothesis Imperiled by Goulder?

Goulder's main challenge to the 2DH is threefold. First, he argues that there is no mention of Q in patristic literature. Of course, in the nineteenth century, Schleiermacher, Lachmann, Credner and Weisse

---

46. See R. W. Funk, *New Gospel Parallels*, vol. 1/2: *Mark* (rev. ed.; Foundations and Facets: Reference Series; Sonoma, Calif.: Polebridge, 1990); and idem, *Poetics of Biblical Narrative* (Sonoma, Calif.; Polebridge, 1988).

47. See V. K. Robbins, *The Tapestry of Early Christian Discourse: Rhetoric, Society and Ideology* (London: Routledge, 1996).

supposed that Papias's *Logia* referred to Q or something very much like Q. But Goulder is quite right to insist that "Papias is sand" (*LNP* 33; "Juggernaut," 669). Indeed. Papias is sand, as Lührmann has most recently shown and as the majority of twentieth-century Synoptic scholars hold.[48] Hence, it is a misrepresentation to assert that "the Q hypothesis rests in part on a misunderstanding" ("Juggernaut," 669), if what is meant is that the hypothesis rests logically on Papias. It does not. A careful reading of Holtzmann shows that, despite the fact that he referred to Q with the siglum L (for Logia), Papias's testimony played no role in the architecture of Holtzmann's argument.[49] In the early twentieth century critics such as W. C. Allen, J. A. Robinson, F. C. Burkitt, B. W. Bacon, and J. C. Hawkins had already rejected the designation Q as "logia" on the grounds that it was question begging.[50] Even those who wished to maintain an Aramaic Q did not found their case on Papias's dubious statements, but on Wellhausen's theory of translation variants.[51]

Goulder also contends that the absence of mentions of Q in patristic sources provides an argument against its existence. Tuckett's point that other documents of the early Jesus movement have gone missing does not, of course, quite meet Goulder's objection. But it is not far off. After all, we know of Paul's "tearful letter" to the Corinthians not because it is listed in some patristic source, but only because of a quite passing comment made by Paul himself. Without this notation, we would have no hint at all of such a letter. Or again: we deduce the existence of a "Two Ways" document, not because it is mentioned in any patristic

48. D. Lührmann, "Q: Sayings of Jesus or Logia?" in *The Gospel behind the Gospels: Current Studies on Q* (ed. R. A. Piper; Novum Testamentum Supplement 75; Leiden: Brill, 1995), 97–116.

49. H. J. Holtzmann, *Die synoptischen Evangelien: Ihr Ursprung und geschichtlicher Charakter* (Leipzig: Engelmann, 1863). See J. S. Kloppenborg Verbin, *Excavating Q: The History and Setting of the Sayings Gospel* (Minneapolis: Fortress; Edinburgh: T&T Clark, 2000), chap. 6.

50. W. C. Allen, "Did St Matthew and St Luke Use the Logia?" *Expository Times* 11 (1899–1900): 424–26, esp. 425; J. A. Robinson, *The Study of the Gospels* (London: Longmans, Green, 1902), 70; F. C. Burkitt, *The Gospel History and Its Transmission* (Edinburgh: T&T Clark, 1906), 127, 130; B. W. Bacon, "A Turning Point in Synoptic Criticism," *Harvard Theological Review* 1 (1908): 48–69; J. C. Hawkins, *Horae Synopticae: Contributions to the Study of the Synoptic Problem* (2d ed.; Oxford: Clarendon, 1909; repr. 1968), 107.

51. E.g., J. C. Hawkins, "Probabilities as to the So-Called Double Tradition of St. Matthew and St. Luke," in *Oxford Studies in the Synoptic Problem* (ed. W. Sanday; Oxford: Clarendon, 1911), 95–140, esp. 104; G. D. Castor, *Matthew's Sayings of Jesus: The Non-Marcan Common Source of Matthew and Luke* (Chicago: University of Chicago Press, 1918), 17–18.

source, but because its existence follows logically from an analysis of the possible literary relationships among the Didache, Barnabas, and the *Doctrina Apostolorum*.[52] Hence, the nonmention of Q in early Christian sources is neither unparalleled nor, under the circumstances, particularly troubling.

Goulder's second objection has to do with the minor agreements. I have already indicated that these can be accommodated on several realistic versions of the 2DH. Of course, they can also be explained on the complex hypotheses of Boismard or on Robert Gundry's view that Luke had some access to Matthew as well as Q,[53] or on the 2GH or FGH.

Goulder's final and most important argument against the existence of Q has to do with the appearance of allegedly Matthean vocabulary in Luke. There are in fact two types of observations.

Goulder argues that some of the minor agreements display characteristically Matthean and clearly un-Lucan vocabulary. If this observation were correct, the 2DH would hardly offer a convenient account. Rather than treating the minor agreements as the coincidental alteration of Mark by Matthew and Luke, it would be more likely that Matthean choices had directly or indirectly influenced Luke.[54] The real difficulty, however, lies with finding such vocabulary. Mark Goodacre, sympathetic to Goulder's thesis, surveys Goulder's candidates and finds that some cannot be considered Matthean on statistical grounds (occurring, for example, only once in Matthew).[55] Tuckett adds that other instances

---

52. See J. S. Kloppenborg, "The Transformation of Moral Exhortation in *Didache* 1–5," in *The Didache in Context: Essays on Its Text, History and Transmission* (ed. C. N. Jefford; Novum Testamentum Supplement 77; Leiden: Brill, 1995), 88–109.

53. R. H. Gundry, "Matthean Foreign Bodies in Agreements of Luke with Matthew against Mark: Evidence That Luke Used Matthew," in *The Four Gospels 1992: Festschrift Frans Neirynck* (ed. F. Van Segbroeck, C. M. Tuckett, G. Van Belle, and J. Verheyden; Bibliotheca ephemeridum theologicarum lovaniensium 100; Leuven: Leuven University Press/Peeters, 1992), 1467–95.

54. Goulder, "Putting Q." Goodacre (*Goulder and the Gospels*, 93–93) notes that Goulder has steadily made this criterion more stringent: in 1978 he looked for non-Lucan words or phrases that were "typical of, or plainly redacted by, Matthew" (219); similarly, "Farrer on Q," *Theology* 83 (1980): 195: "in some way characteristic of Matthew" and "in some way uncharacteristic of Luke." In "Luke's Knowledge of Matthew," 144, Goulder drops "in some way" from this criterion. Tuckett ("Relationship between Matthew and Luke," 130) agrees with the final formulation: "The Matthew-Luke agreement must be both positively Matthean and positively un-Lukan."

55. (a) Matt 4:13 || Luke 4:16 (*Nazara*) against Mark 1:14; see Goulder, "Putting Q," 219–21; Tuckett, "Relationship between Matthew and Luke," 131; Goodacre, *Goulder and the Gospels*, 101–2. The International Q Project argues that the MA is due to Q: S. Carruth and J. M. Robinson, *Q 4:1– 13, 16* (ed. C. Heil; Documenta Q; Leuven: Peeters, 1996), 391–442; (b) Matt 26:68 || Luke 22:64

are not un-Lucan and others still are thoroughly Lucan.[56] Goodacre finds six instances of Matthean/un-Lucan vocabulary among the minor agreements.[57] But he also finds two instances of un-Matthean/Lucan vocabulary.[58] Goodacre seems to take this as a matter of democracy, the Matthean vocabulary winning in a vote against the Lucan; but such a conclusion is dubious from a logical point of view. Moreover, the entire approach is weakened by the definition of Matthean/un-Lucan.

Goulder argues that Luke's use of the phrase *their synagogues* in a summary statement in Luke 4:15 reflects Matthew's (redactional) usage in Matt 13:54 (in a the story of Jesus' visit to Nazareth), where Mark has only the word *synagogue*. It is true that Matthew uses the phrase *their synagogues* five times (three times redactionally). Mark uses the phrase twice (1:23, 39). On any accounting, Luke's treatment of Mark 1:14–28 is complicated. Luke omitted Mark 1:15–20, substituted his own story of the visit to Nazara for one that occurred much later in Mark (6:1–6a), and created an introduction (Luke 4:14b–15) and summary (4:37) from elements in Mark 1:21, 23, 28:

(*paisas* and *tis estin*) against Mark 14:65; see Goulder, "Putting Q," 226–28; Tuckett, "Relationship between Matthew and Luke," 136–37; Goodacre, *Goulder and the Gospels*, 102–5, who notes that *paiō* appears only once in Matthew and Luke, and *tis estin* occurs not only in Matthew (redactionally), but in Mark (5 times) and 13 times in Luke (5 times redactionally).

56. Tuckett, "Relationship between Matthew and Luke," 132–40:

Matt 9:2 ‖ Luke 5:18 (*epi klinēs*) against Mark 2:3 (*krabbatos*)

Matt 17:5 ‖ Luke 9:34 (*epeskiasen* [Luke: *epeskiazein*] *autous*) against Mark 9:7 (*episkiazousa autois*)

Matt 27:1 ‖ Luke 22:66 (*presbyteroi* [Luke: *presbyterion*] *tou laou*) against Mark 15:1 (*presbyterōn*)

Matt 27:58–59 ‖ Luke 23:52–53 (*houtos proselthōn tō pilatō ētēsato . . . enetylixen auto . . . kai ethēken auton*) against Mark 15:43–46 (*eisēlthen pros ton pilaton kai ētēsato . . . eneilēsen . . . kai ethēken auton*)

Matt 28:1 ‖ Luke 23:54 (*epiphōskein*) against Mark 16:1

57. Goodacre, *Goulder and the Gospels*, 107–17:

Matt 12:15 ‖ Luke 6:17 (*pantas*) against Mark 3:7

Matt 8:27 ‖ Luke 8:25 (*hypakouousin*) against Mark 4:41 (*hypakouei*)

Matt 13:54 ‖ Luke 4:15–16 (*synagōgē* [Luke: *synagōgais*] *autōn*) against Mark 6:2 (*synagōgē*)

Matt 14:13 ‖ Luke 9:11 (*hoi* [Luke + *de*] *ochloi ēkolouthēsan*) against Mark 6:33

Matt 12:27 ‖ Luke 20:32 (*hysteron*) against Mark 12:22 (*eschaton*)

Matt 26:47 (*idou . . . ēlthen*) ‖ Luke 22:47 (*idou . . . proērcheto*) against Mark 14:43 (*paraginetai*)

58. Goodacre, *Goulder and the Gospels*, 117–22:

Matt 14:21 ‖ Luke 9:14 (*hōsei*) against Mark 6:44

Matt 22:35 ‖ Luke 10:25 (*nomikos peirazōn* [Luke: *ekpeirazōn*] *didaskale*) against Mark 12:28

Mark 1	**Luke 4**
[14]Now after John was arrested, Jesus came to the Galilee....	[14]Then Jesus, filled with the power of the Spirit, returned to the Galilee and a report about him spread through the entire region.
	[15]He taught in their synagogues and was praised by everyone.
(6:1–6a)	4:16–30
1:15–20	no parallels
[21]And they entered Capernaum; and on the Sabbath he entered the synagogue and taught.	[31]And he went down to Capernaum, a city of the Galilee, and was teaching them on the Sabbath.
[22]And they were astounded at his teaching because he was teaching them as one having authority not like the scribes.	[32]And they were astounded at his teaching because he spoke with authority.
[23]And just then in their synagogue there was a man with an unclean spirit....	[33]And in the synagogue there was a man who had the spirit of an unclean demon....
[28]And at once his fame spread throughout the entire region of the Galilee....	[37]And a report about him reached every place in the region.

Matthew's phrase in 13:54 ("he came to his hometown and began to teach the people in their synagogue") is a simple adaptation of Mark 6:1–2 ("he left ... and came to his hometown, ... and ... on the Sabbath he began to teach in the synagogue"). But Luke does not take over Mark's Nazareth story (6:1–6a) and shows no affinities with Matt 13:54–58, apart from the proverb (Matt 13:57b = Mark 6:4), which in any case is quoted in a form that does not correspond with either Matthew or Mark (or John 4:44). Instead, Luke depends on other sources for his Nazara story and takes from the Markan context the elements that he uses in Luke 4:14b–15, 37. One hardly needs to appeal to Matt 13:54 in order to account for "in their synagogues" in Luke 4:15; it is better explained as the result of the reconfiguration of Markan materials. Conversely, to derive the phrase from Matthew then leaves us wondering why Luke failed to take over any of the other features of the Matthean

Nazareth pericope.[59] Moreover, as Tuckett points out, Luke uses the phrase "synagogue of the Jews" in Acts. Hence it is hardly warranted to insist that Luke took his pronoun from Matthew when it was available in the immediate Markan context as well.

Or again: Luke's use of the biblicizing *idou* at 22:47 is declared to be Matthean. But this is done only by narrowing the statistics to include only the usages of the particle after an absolute genitive (eleven times in Matthew [four times in Matt[Red]]; once in Luke).[60] But *idou* is common in all three Synoptics (Matt 62 times, Mark 17 times, Luke 57 times) and is added by Luke Mark four times where Matthew does not have it and seven times where Matthew also adds the word.[61] The situation is complex: *idou* is a Septuagintalism that occurs 1,074 times; Luke is known to imitate Septuagintal style; and he adds *idou* to Mark eleven times (including the four times where Matthew does not have the word). It seems rather dubious to ignore Markan usage, Luke's preferences (quite independent of Matthew), or Septuagintal usage when accounting for the agreement with Matthew at Luke 22:47.

The second form of Goulder's argument is similar. He argues that the presence of "many rare and striking phrases in Q that are also favorite expressions of Matthew" indicates that what is usually assigned to Q is in fact Matthean ("Juggernaut," 672). This is a form of the argument first articulated in 1843 by Eduard Zeller, who argued that when a word or phrase appeared in gospel A only where gospel B also evidenced it, but at several other points in gospel B, it was a valid inference that A used B.[62]

---

59. Goulder (*LNP* 299–300) agrees that Luke 4:14 (*kai phēmē exēlthen kath' holēs tēs perichōrou peri autou*) is taken from Mark 1:28 but does not notice that *in their synagogue* occurs also in Mark 1:23. Instead, he argues that Luke "unintentionally" carried over *their* from Matt 13:54.

60. Superscript [Red] means redactional and superscript [S] refers to texts appearing only in one Gospel.

61. Neirynck, *Minor Agreements*, 273–74.

62. E. Zeller, "Studien zur neutestamentlichen Theologie 4: Vergleichende Übersicht über den Wörtervorrath der neutestamentlichen Schriftsteller," *Theologische Jahrbücher* (Tübingen) 2 (1843): 443–543, esp. 527–31. Zeller's results were mixed, with seventy-eight words and phrases allegedly supporting Matthean priority and thirty-one supporting Markan priority. Despite the seemingly inconclusive nature of his statistics, Zeller declared that an "overburdening proportion" (532) favored Matthew. C. M. Tuckett ("The Griesbach Hypothesis in the 19th Century," *Journal for the Study of the New Testament* 3 [1979], 29–60, 69 n. 57) notes that Zeller's list includes many instances where a word that occurs once in Mark and twice in Matthew or twice in Mark and three times in Matthew is declared to be characteristically Matthean.

Goulder's "many" is rather an exaggeration; he mentions the following items:

oligopistoi (Q 12:28 + Matt 8:26[Red]; 14:31[Red]; 16:8[Red])

ekei estai ho klauthmos kai ho brygmos tōn odontōn (Q 13:28 + Matt 13:42[S], 50[S]; 22:13[S]; 25:51[Red]?, 30[S])

the concluding formula of Matthew's sermons (which does not appear in Luke [cf. Luke 7:1a])

gennēmata echidnōn (Q 3:7 + Matt 12:34[Red]?; 23:33[Red]?)

poiein karpon (Q 3:8–9; 6:43 [twice] + Matt 7:17[Red], 19[Red]?; 13:26[S]; 21:43[Red])

ekkoptetai kai eis pyr balletai (Q 3:9 + Matt 7:19[Red])

synagagein ton siton eis tēn apothēkēn autou (Q 3:17; 12:24 + Matt 13:30[Red]; Luke 12:18)

Goulder's definition of Matthean and semi-Matthean vocabulary is highly problematic, but even so, Goodacre's sympathetic analysis shows that Q pericopes also contain Lucan, un-Matthean, and semi-Lucan words.[63] Presumably Goulder accounts for these by understanding the semi-Lucan words as "Luke-pleasing" words that Luke took over from Matthew and enhanced. The Lucan, un-Matthean words pose a more serious problem for Goulder's thesis since, by the logic of his own argument, they should lead to the conclusion that Matthew used Luke. In fact, most of the semi-Lucan and semi-Matthean words could just as easily be treated as Q vocabulary embraced by Luke and Matthew, respectively, and the Lucan, un-Matthean and Matthean, un-Lucan words as Q vocabulary taken over by Luke and Matthew less "enthusiastically." Moreover, the obvious Mattheanisms such as *hē basileia tōn ouranōn* (Matt: 32x) are wholly lacking in minimal Q or in Luke.

The general difficulty with the argument is that it can hardly exclude the possibility that a singly or doubly attested word in gospel A (Q)

---

63. Goodacre, *Goulder and the Gospels*, 42–88.

appealed to the author of gospel B (Matthew), who expanded its usage. This is precisely the point made by Goulder against Farmer's reiteration of Zeller's argument.[64] Yet as Tuckett points out, Goulder himself uses the argument that he declared to be fallacious in his 1989 book on Luke.[65] Since Zeller's principle is reversible, it is invalid for determining the direction of dependence.

Conclusion

In this essay I have argued, first, that Goulder has adopted a view of paradigms that corresponds more closely to Popper's view of scientific theories than it does to Kuhn's. The significance of this observation lies in the fact that it seems apparent that Goulder's interlocutors do not share his rather strict Popperian view of falsification. Moreover, I have argued that whatever its applicability to hypotheses in the experimental sciences, Popper's view is inappropriate when it comes to the study of the Synoptic Problem. In place of a schematic and easily falsifiable model of Synoptic interrelationships, I have argued for a historically and technically realistic view. To adopt such a view, as I believe that most proponents do, renders ineffective most of the arguments that Goulder mounts against the 2DH.

Second, I have suggested that Goulder's own view is not a paradigm, at least by Kuhn's standards. It fits easily within the broad paradigm of Gospels studies that has prevailed since the early 1800s. This paradigm

---

64. See W. R. Farmer, "Certain Results Reached by Sir John C. Hawkins and C. F. Burney Which Make More Sense If Luke Knew Matthew," in *Synoptic Studies: The Ampleforth Conferences of 1982 and 1983* (ed. C. M. Tuckett; Journal for the Study of the New Testament Supplement 7; Sheffield: JSOT Press, 1984), 75–98; and Goulder's reply (100): "But [Farmer's argument] is a fallacy. A's favorite expressions may not have appealed to B; indeed they may be classified as favorite *because* they did not appeal to B. Sometimes later B may copy in expressions of earlier A inadvertently; and sometimes a casual expression of earlier A may appeal strongly to B so that he uses it often." Goulder then notes that he has taken over some of Farrer's favorite phrases, some inadvertently, others used more often. He continues: "I do not wish to seem hard on Farmer, as I made virtually the same error of method myself in a paper to the SNTS seminar in 1981, where Farmer was present. Three of my instances of 'inadvertent' carrying over of a characteristic Matthean phrase by Luke were on Hawkin's list on pp. 170–71: 'you generation of vipers!,' 'there shall be weeping and gnashing of teeth,' 'and it came to pass when Jesus finished these sayings.' They might just be Q phrases that Matthew liked very much; though there are other reasons in fact for preferring the inadvertence explanation, which I offered."

65. Tuckett, "Existence of Q," 35–36.

privileges the Gospels in their historical, literary, and socio-rhetorical particularity and seeks to establish a plausible theory of literary dependence. Formally speaking, Goulder's hypothesis is no different from the 2DH, the 2GH, or the several more complex hypotheses that are advocated today although, to be sure, Goulder has several interestingly different emphases in his explanatory theory.

Finally, I have argued that none of Goulder's points raised against the 2DH is especially telling. This is either because a realistic model of the 2DH can accommodate the few problematic minor agreements without collapsing or because the evidence that Goulder adduces of Mattheanisms in Luke (or Q) is both weak and admits of counter-evidence: Lucanisms in Matthew.

Reflection on Goulder's hypothesis and its reception raises an interesting puzzle. Goulder has not been successful in offering decisive objections to the 2DH,[66] but even if he has not, it is a perfectly rational option to embrace his hypothesis, since it provides a ready solution to the issue of the minor agreements and the allegedly Matthean vocabulary in Luke. It is possible to account for Lucanisms in Matthew by his notion of "Luke-pleasing" vocabulary. To be sure, there are some serious technical problems involved in rendering his thesis plausible, notably accounting for Luke's almost complete detachment of the double tradition from the context in which he found it in Matthew and his relocation of that material elsewhere, or the puzzle that, when faced with material common to Mark and Matthew, Luke never prefers Matthew's sequence over Mark's and almost never prefers Matthew's wording to Mark's.

It might be that resistance to the FGH comes down to the inability of exegetes to imagine such activities on Luke's part. But I doubt it. I think it rather more likely that ideological factors are at play. For much of its history, Q has served as a way to bridge the gap between Matthew

---

66. Goulder seems to concede this point, though he has varying explanations. In "Farrer on Q," 194, his explanation is *ad hominem:* "Q is not going to collapse: it has the highest vested interest of any New Testament hypothesis in that virtually ever scholar has written a book assuming its truth." Elsewhere ("Luke's Knowledge of Matthew," 144–45), his explanation has more to do with the nature of refutation: "In matters of this kind we cannot hope for proof. The four hypotheses [2DH, 2GH, FGH, and Deutero-Markan theory] are in competition with one another in plausibility. The Two-Source hypothesis starts with the tremendous advantage of having been widely taught as *the* solution for at least fifty years."

and Luke in the 80s or 90s and the historical Jesus. Harnack believed Q to be a largely unadulterated collection of Jesus sayings. And despite the fact that most of the technical studies that have appeared on Q since Hoffmann's 1972 Habilitationsschrift have tried to treat Q primarily as a document in its own right rather than as a source for the historical Jesus, outside of these specialist circles, Q is still regularly thought to offer immediate or near immediate access to Jesus.[67] Hence John P. Meier dismisses quickly studies that attempt to ascertain a composition history of Q as "hypothetical" — what in New Testament studies do we do that is not hypothetical? — and satisfies himself with the caricature of Q as a "grab bag."[68] This allows him to use Q pretty much as Harnack had done and to quarry Q for Jesus tradition without having to inquire whether Q's own editorializing and creativity renders those excavations problematic.

If theories of the stratification of Q have been regarded as imperiling the quest of the historical Jesus, Goulder's thesis would have a yet more devastating effect. Not only is most of the double tradition treated as the result of Matthean editorial activity, but the special Lucan material, including the parables of the man going down the road and the lost son, so central to many constructions of the historical Jesus, would dissolve into Luke's exegetical imagination.

An examination of the history of solutions to the Synoptic puzzles can show how rather technical, almost algebraic, solutions to literary puzzles have functioned within broader theological paradigms and have been embraced not so much because they solved literary problems, but because they seemed to provide literary models that cohered with broader ideological interests. This is true of the use of the Griesbach hypothesis by F. C. Baur and his associates; and it is true of the use of the Markan hypothesis by liberal theology up to Harnack. The 2DH is difficult to displace not only because it still serves as an effective compositional

---

67. P. Hoffmann, *Studien zur Theologie der Logienquelle* (Neutestamentliche Abhandlungen n.s. 8; Münster: Aschendorff, 1972; 2d ed. in 1975; 3d ed. in 1980).

68. J. P. Meier, *A Marginal Jew: Rethinking the Historical Jesus*, vol. 2: *Mentor, Message, and Miracles* (Anchor Bible Reference Library; New York: Doubleday, 1994), 179–81. Meier's characterization of Q as a grab bag without a coherent theology or a supporting community allows him to prescind from the literary and historical questions of its origin, tradents, and editorial tendencies, and to use Q simply as a "distinct and valuable source for sayings of Jesus and John."

hypothesis and because compelling counterevidence has not been produced; but it also allows for a relatively fulsome picture of Jesus and seems to lend support to general theological models concerning the gradual development and articulation of christological, eschatological, and ecclesiological doctrines.

In order for the FGH to be an effective counterforce to the 2DH, it is necessary to show not only that it solves literary puzzles more effectively than the 2DH, but that it holds the promise of addressing larger theoretical issues raised in the dominant paradigm, such as the relationship of the historical Jesus to the pictures of Jesus in the early Jesus movement and a comprehensive theory of the creation, use, and transmission of early Christian texts.[69]

---

69. A shorter and slightly different version of this paper appeared as "Is There a New Paradigm?" in *Christology, Controversy, and Community: New Testament Essays in Honour of David Catchpole* (ed. D. Horrell and C. M. Tuckett; Supplements to Novum Testamentum 99; Leiden: Brill, 2000), 23–47.

GRECO-ROMAN WRITING PRACTICES AND LUKE'S GOSPEL

Revisiting "The Order of a Crank"

Robert A. Derrenbacker Jr.

With this volume, we are honoring Michael Goulder and his important contribution to the ongoing scholarly discussion of the Synoptic Problem.[1] One reason, I think, that the Synoptic Problem remains a "problem" has to do with most scholars' unimaginative and anachronistic conceptions of the Synoptic evangelists as first-century writers in the Greco-Roman world. Most Synoptic source critics seem to imagine a literary world for the Gospel writers characterized by extensive literacy, ample access to writing materials, the proliferation of writing desks that allow an author to have visual contact with written sources, and, generally, a conception of a literary environment not too different from our own age of information technology.

Goulder's own work provides a partial exception to this trend. For example, in suggesting the rabbinic technique of midrash as a way to understand Matthew's compositional program, Goulder promotes a specific compositional method indigenous to the Jewish world of the Greco-Roman era. In addition, as part of his new paradigm on Luke, Goulder extensively discusses Luke's treatment of Matthew with an

---

1. This essay is taken from a portion of the chapter entitled "The Farrer-Goulder Hypothesis" in my forthcoming book *Ancient Compositional Practices and the Synoptic Problem* (BETL; Leuven: Peeters, 2003).

eye on the actual mechanics of Luke's use of Matthew's (and Mark's) scroll(s) in a rather cramped study.

Few Synoptic source critics describe what Luke is mechanically doing with the same regular and meticulous detail as Goulder.[2] He is to be commended for his minority position in Synoptic Problems discussions in that he, in a limited fashion, attempts to describe what Matthew and Luke are doing in terms of the literary worlds of the first century. We, of course, should not be surprised that Goulder takes the minority view. And given that I am both an advocate of the Two-Source theory and a member of the International Q Project, I would like to both discuss and challenge Goulder's description of Luke's use of Matthew.

We begin in 1924, when B. H. Streeter stated in his seminal work *The Four Gospels* that it was untenable to think that Luke had direct access to the written text of Matthew. Streeter argued that if

> Luke derived this material [which we call Q on the Two-Source theory] from Matthew, he must have gone through both Matthew and Mark so as to discriminate with meticulous precision between Marcan and non-Marcan material; he must then have proceeded with the utmost care to tear every little piece of non-Marcan material he desired to use from the context of Mark in which it appeared in Matthew — in spite of the fact that contexts in Matthew are always exceedingly appropriate — in order to re-insert it into a different context of Mark having no special appropriateness. A theory which would make an author capable of such a proceeding would only be tenable if, on other grounds, we had reason to believe he was a crank.[3]

Some sixty years later, Goulder published an essay entitled "The Order of a Crank." There, Goulder attempts to make a cogent case for the order of Luke, Goulder's "crank," to use Streeter's terminology, concluding that "Luke's knowledge of Matthew seems to be multiply confirmed, and his

---

2. These efforts are rather pointedly critiqued by F. G. Downing, "A Paradigm Perplex: Luke, Matthew and Mark," *New Testament Studies* 38 (1992): 15–36. In response to Downing, Goulder offers some deserved criticism and defense of his paradigm in "Luke's Compositional Options," *New Testament Studies* 39 (1993): 150–52.

3. B. H. Streeter, *The Four Gospels: A Study of Origins* (London: Macmillan, 1924), 183.

ordering of Matthew shown to be, on the whole, careful, rational and indeed sophisticated," proposing that "Canon Streeter owes St Luke an apology."[4] In this essay, I will focus on a critical analysis of Goulder's description of Luke's compositional methods in light of what we know about the ways in which ancient authors worked with and treated their source materials, specifically at Luke 13:22–18:8. But first, I turn to Goulder's general description of Luke's compositional procedure.

Goulder's Picture of Luke's Compositional Procedure

Goulder describes Luke as a "harmonist" who was "concerned to get his order right."[5] But unlike "modern harmonists," Luke's technique is distinct in at least four areas: (1) "[It] is not so important [for Luke] for teaching material to be in order as for the incidents [i.e., narrative material]."[6] (2) Luke often "break[s] up long units of teaching material [from Matthew] into more manageable sections."[7] (3) Since "Luke's policy" is "to take Mark in large sections … without intrusions from Matthew, then of necessity he will have to have the non-Marcan material out of the Marcan context."[8] (4) Luke's procedure is not at all like Streeter's picture of Luke "conflating" Mark and Q, where he takes "a phrase from here, a word from there."[9] Instead, Luke adopts the policy of following one source at a time, seen in Goulder's imaginary picture of Luke the writer:

> My Luke has probably a cramped writing table with space for his own scroll and the one he is using as his base-of-the-moment. Mark and Matthew take turns to go on the floor. Where there are overlaps and minor agreements and such things, it is from reminiscence of a familiar parallel text.[10]

---

4. Goulder, "Crank," 130.
5. Ibid., 112. Cf. Luke 1:1–4.
6. Ibid., 112.
7. Ibid., 112. The example given by Goulder is Luke's abbreviation of Mark 4:1–34 into fifteen verses in Luke 8:4–18.
8. Ibid., 112.
9. Ibid., 112–13.
10. Ibid., 113.

Thus, four important details regarding Luke's compositional procedure can be drawn from this description: (1) Goulder imagines Luke working with one source at a time; (2) the medium of Luke's sources, as well as his text, is the scroll; (3) Luke is using a writing table that is able to accommodate both his text and the particular exemplar he is using at the time; and (4) Luke will often rely on his memory while having visual contact with his exemplar in the production of his Gospel.

Goulder outlines Luke's procedure as a harmonist of sorts who works with one source at a time:

Lucan Pericopes	Source
Jesus' infancy through the temptation (1:1–4:13)	Matthew
Jesus' early Galilean ministry (4:14–6:19)	Mark
Sermon on the Plain through the description of Jesus' female disciples (6:20–8:3)	Matthew
parable of the sower to just prior to Luke's travel narrative (8:4–9:50)	Mark
travel narrative (9:51–18:8)	Matthew[11]
passion narrative (18:9–24:53)	Mark[12]

Otherwise, when Luke is following Mark and occasionally incorporates Matthean wording (or vice versa), he is simply recalling his "source on the floor" through reminiscence.[13]

In light of this summary of Goulder's description of Luke's compositional practices, a number of items become apparent. First, Goulder's Luke generally follows either Matthew or Mark for extended periods of time: Matthew's Gospel takes its place on Luke's table on at least three occasions, as does Mark. Second, it is also clear that, when Mark takes its place on Luke's table, Luke generally follows the Markan order closely,

---

11. Luke uses Matt 13–23 in reverse in Luke 13:22–18:8.

12. For the parable of the pounds (Luke 19:11–27) and the judging of the twelve tribes of Israel (22:29–30), Luke turns again to Matthew.

13. Again, "Where there are overlaps and minor agreements and such things, it is from reminiscence of a familiar parallel text" (Goulder, "Crank," 113). An example of this phenomenon would be the infamous minor agreement between Matthew and Luke in the episode of Peter's denial: *kai exelthōn exō eklausen pikrōs* (Matt 26:75 || Luke 22:62). Here, Goulder argues that Luke is following Mark, yet opts for Matthew's wording even though Matthew's scroll is presently on the floor of Luke's study (*LNP* 749–50). See also the parable of the mustard seed and leaven (Luke 13:18–21), about which Goulder states (*LNP* 566) that Luke "opts for the Matthean version," yet "an echo of Mark's parable rings in his [Luke's] mind, with its double question opening, 'How are we to liken the kingdom of God, and in what parable shall we set it?' (4:30)."

especially from Mark 4 onward. However, when Luke is following Matthew, Luke is quite prone to reorder the Matthean pericopes, especially in Luke 9:51–18:8. Again, Goulder's explanation for this phenomenon is that it "is not so important for teaching material to be in order as for the incidents"; thus, Luke "break[s] up long units of [Matthew's] teaching material into more manageable sections."[14]

Luke's Compositional Procedure at 13:22–18:8

Description

Goulder's description of Luke's compositional procedure at Luke 13:22–18:8 is both particularly unique and quite interesting. Here, Goulder imagines Luke working backward through the scroll of his Matthean exemplar. It is a scenario that Goulder first described in 1984:

> According to our hypothesis, Luke has [up to 13:21] ... run through the non-Marcan sections of Matthew [1–12 and 23–25]. Sometimes he has copied the material word for word (especially in the early sections, the Baptist's Sermon and Temptations); sometimes he has emended freely, so much so that we need our Ariadne's thread to find our way through the labyrinth after him. But he has gone through Matt. 1–12 and 23–25, we may feel, carefully and in order, even if he has made a number of surprising omissions. And now, dear reader, you are St Luke, and there is the scroll of Matthew on the table before you, and the rolled up portion is Matt. 1–25, and the next words in Matt. 26 open the Passion narrative. You are aware that you have not even been through Matt. 13–22 for non-Marcan gems: what would be your policy? Well, I hope you will not think me a crank for suggesting it; but the obvious move seems to me *to go back through the rolled up scroll and to take the missing pieces as they come, backward* [in Luke 13:22–18:8]. It is true that this will involve sacrificing the principle of order; but then Luke has only teaching, no incidents, to concern himself with in the gleaning process — and in fact his leap from Matt. 12 to

---

14. Goulder, "Crank," 112.

Matt. 23 necessarily involved gleaning in some form, and therefore the sacrifice of the Matthean order *in toto*.[15]

Goulder argues that this is a "psychologically believable" process,[16] one that he illustrates in 1989 (*LNP* 582) and reproduced in table 1 (pp. 70–71). The table does not include "all the references," states Goulder, "but they are the most obvious ones, and almost all of them are Mt.R. [= Matthean redaction]. Their combined impact makes a Lucan policy of reverse gleaning through Matthew 25–16 very probable" (*LNP* 582).

Thus, I would like to take up in turn several of Goulder's points regarding the compositional scenario he images for Luke, particularly at 13:22–18:8.

Writing Tables

Modern writers are very familiar with desks as writing and working surfaces, usually standing thirty inches or so off the ground. The picture of this working environment is one where a writer spreads his/her work out on desks or writing tables and works in an environment of controlled chaos as letters, essays, and articles are composed on paper or computer, surrounded by stacks of books, notes, and journals. However, ancient writers and scribes, of course, did not work in this fashion. We know from both artistic depictions of ancient authors and from a few literary sources that writing desks did not come into use until sometime after the fourth century c.e., finally gaining popularity by the eighth and ninth centuries c.e.[17] The posture of scribes and writers in antiquity was either squatting, with one's tunic stretched over one's knees creating a crude but efficient writing surface, or seated on a stool or a bench with the writing surface (usually a scroll) propped up on one knee, which could be supported by a stool. Occasionally, a writer might stand if he or she were working with a small codex that could be supported in one hand.

---

15. Ibid., 121 (emphasis original).
16. Ibid., 129.
17. These various depictions are discussed in some detail in B. M. Metzger, "When Did Scribes Begin to Use Writing Desks?" in *Historical and Literary Studies: Pagan and Jewish Christian* (Grand Rapids: Eerdmans, 1968), 123–37.

In addition, there are a few pieces of literary evidence that support the idea of writing without the assistance of tables and desks. Several ancient and Byzantine colophons discuss the participation of the scribe's knees in the production of texts. For example, a third-century C.E. colophon from a copy of Homer's *Iliad* reads as follows: "I am the conclusion [of the written work], the guardian of scribes. The pen wrote me, [as did the] right hand and knee."[18] In light of this phenomenon, G. M. Parássoglou writes the following regarding scribal posture in antiquity and the cumbersome nature of scrolls: "Writing on a papyrus roll placed on one's lap was indubitably a difficult task and, regardless of the expertise that many of the ancient scribes may have reached..., must have placed serious limitations on what could be achieved."[19]

By now, the implications to our understanding of the physical conditions under which the ancient writers worked should be manifest. With scribal posture, many wrongly imagine that ancient writers worked in an environment similar to our own literary culture. All the main "solutions" to the Synoptic Problem have proponents who are guilty of inaccurately picturing the evangelists as writers working without a writing desk, but as authors seated behind spacious (and sometimes elaborate) writing surfaces.[20] Thus, I would like to challenge Goulder to "redraw" his picture of Luke's study in light of the nonuse of writing tables in antiquity.

The Use of "Memory" in Literary Productions

While much of Luke's source in 13:22–18:8 is a sort of "reverse contextualization" of Matt 16–25, Goulder's Luke often draws from elsewhere in Matthew "by reminiscence" (*LNP* 581). In fact, the use of memory is a consistent practice of Goulder's Luke elsewhere in his Gospel.

---

18. See G. M. Parássoglou, "ΔΕΞΙΑ ΧΕΙΡ ΚΑΙ ΓΟΝΥ: Some Thoughts on the Postures of the Ancient Greeks and Romans When Writing on Papyrus Rolls," *Scrittura e Civiltà* 3 (1979): 5–22.

19. Ibid., 20.

20. See, e.g., B. L. Mack's comments regarding Mark: "[Mark's Gospel] was composed at a desk in a scholar's study lined with texts and open to discourse with other intellectuals. In Mark's study were chains of miracle stories, collections of pronouncement stories in various states of elaboration, some form of Q, memos on parables and proof texts, the Scriptures, including the prophets, written materials from the Christ cult, and other literature representative of Hellenistic Judaism. It would not be unthinkable that Mark had a copy of the Wisdom of Solomon, or some of the Maccabean literature, or some Samaritan texts, and so on"; *A Myth of Innocence: Mark and Christian Origins* (Philadelphia: Fortress, 1988), 322–23.

Table 1
Luke 13:22–18:8 || Matt 25–16 (Second Half of the Journey)
(Goulder, *LNP* 571–64)

Subsection	Unit Title	Luke	Visual Contact with Matthew
41. Israel and the Gentiles (Luke 13:22–14:24)	Condemnation of Israel	13:22–35	25:10–12 (26:1–2)[a] 23:37–39
	Dropsical Man	14:1–14	23:2, 4, 6, 12 22:1–14
	Great Dinner	14:15–24	22:1–14
42. Cost of Discipleship (Luke 14:25–16:13)	Leaving All	14:25–35	21:33–46
	Joy at Repentance	15:1–32	21:28–32 18:10–14
	Unjust Steward	16:1–13	(18:23–35)
43. Law and the Gospel (Luke 16:14–17:19)	Dives and Lazarus	16:14–31	(18:23–35) 19:24[b]
	Faithfulness	17:1–10	18:6b 18:6a
	Ten Lepers	17:11–19	17:22 17:9, 14 17:15
44. Coming of the Son of Man (Luke 17:20–18:8)	Son of Man's Day	17:20–37	16:1–4 16:21–28
	Unjust Judge	18:1–8	16:27–28

a. *LNP* 576.   b. Goulder, "Crank," 125.

Table 1 (continued)
Luke 13:22–18:8 ‖ Matt 25–16 (Second Half of the Journey)
(Goulder, *LNP* 571–64)

	Matthean Texts by Reminiscence	Other Parallels	Luke's Sources on the Two-Source Theory
41.	Matt 9:35 Matt 7:13–14 Matt 7:22–23[c] Matt 24:43(?)[d] Matt 8:11–12 Matt 20:16[e] Matt 14:1–14	Mark 10:31 Matt 19:27–30 Matt 8:11–12 Matt 19:30	Q 13:24 (25) 26– 27, 28–30 L (=Luke 13:31–33) Q 13:34–35
	Matt 12:9–13	Mark 3:1–6	Q 14:11
			Q 14:16–24
42.	Matt 10:37 Matt 16:24 Matt 19:29 Matt 22:7 Mark 9:50 Matt 5:13	Mark 8:34–35 Mark 9:49–50 Mark 10:29–30 Matt 10:38–39 Matt 16:24–25 John 12:25	Q 14:26–27 Q 14:34–35
			Q 15:4–7 [Q 15:8–10] L (=Luke 15:11–32)
	Matt 6:24		L (=Luke 16:1–12) Q 16:13
43.	Matt 5:20 Matt 11:12–13[f] Matt 11:5 Matt 4:17 Matt 5:20 Matt 5:18 Matt 19:24 Matt 5:32 Matt 19:9 Matt 15:27[g]	Mark 10:11–12	L (=Luke 16:14–15) Q 16:16–18 L (= Luke 16:19–31)
	Matt 21:21 Matt 15:13	Mark 9:28–29, 42 Mark 11:22–23	Q 17:1b–2 Q 17:3b–4 Q 17:6b L (= Luke 17:7–10)
	Matt 8:1–13		L (= Luke 17:11–19
44.	Matt 24:23–24 Matt 24:26–28 Matt 24:37–39 Matt 24:40 Matt 24:17–18 Matt 24:40–41 Matt 24:28	Matt 10:39 Mark 13:15–16, 21–23	[Q 17:20b–21] Q 17:23–37b
	Matt 24:44–46		L (= Luke 18:1–8)

c. Goulder states that Luke "cites" Matt 7:23 (*LNP* 576).
d. *LNP* 573.   e. *LNP* 575.   f. *LNP* 629.   g. *LNP* 634.

For example, the so-called "minor agreements" between Matthew and Luke against Mark in the triple tradition are created when Luke "stick[s] to what Mark says on the scroll in front of him, while allowing the parallel Matthean account to influence him from memory" (*LNP* 428). Also, on at least one occasion, the memory of the "text-on-the-floor" "draws Luke's mind away from" the text in front of him (*LNP* 521).

The study of the role that memory plays in literary compositions of ancient authors has been seldom explored, despite the frequent reference to the procedure by Greco-Roman writers. Jocelyn Penny Small, in her important book *Wax Tablets of the Mind*,[21] offers one of the few studies on the role that memory plays in the composition of texts in the ancient world. Small, an archeologist with an interest in cognitive psychology, argues that in antiquity memory functioned as a repository or storehouse of information, much in the same way we use memory in contemporary culture. However, the ancients differed from us in one very important way: While writers in the contemporary literary world of the West tend to organize their thoughts visually and tangibly through the use of 3" x 5" cards and the like, the ancients instead often used their memories for the organization of the data stored therein. For example, Cicero states that one's memory is "the treasure-house of all things" (*On the Orator* 1.18); it is "the guardian of all parts of rhetoric" and "the treasure-house of ideas supplied by invention" (*Ad Herennium* 3.16.28). As well, Cicero describes his searching the repository of his memory as much like flower picking:

> When the inclination arose in my mind to write a text-book of rhetoric, I did not set before myself one model which I thought necessary to reproduce in all details, of whatever sort they might be, but after collecting all the works on the subject I excerpted what seemed the most suitable precepts from each, and so culled the flower of many minds. (*On Invention* 2.4)

Thus, Small draws the following picture from her study of memory by classical writers: "One extracts some thought, idea, or fact from a larger

---

21. J. P. Small, *Wax Tablets of the Mind: Cognitive Studies of Memory and Literacy in Classical Antiquity* (London: Routledge, 1997).

[written] work and deposits it in one's own storehouse, that is, memory, from which it can be recalled whenever needed, like withdrawing money from a treasury."[22]

Small concludes that ancient writers, before beginning their writing, would "go over all the relevant sources," followed by a combination of those sources into a "new whole," keeping "items separate."[23] This was necessary "for retrieval, since according to the art of memory each item is stored in its own place."[24] Again, while both ancient and modern writers utilize their memories for retrieval of data, ancient writers evidently differ from modern in terms of using memory for the organization of this data.[25]

Goulder's picture of Luke's use of his memory in the production of his Gospel is generally supported by the work of C. B. R. Pelling on Plutarch's use of memory. Based on his careful study of Plutarch, Pelling argued that an ancient author

> would generally choose just one work to have before his eyes when he composed, and this work would provide the basis of his narrative. . . . Items from the earlier reading would more widely be combined with the principal source, but a writer would not normally refer back to that reading to verify individual references, and would instead rely on his memory, or on the briefest of notes. Alternatively, it may be that an author, immediately before narrating an episode would *re*-read one account, and compose with that version fresh in mind. . . . Stray facts and additions would be recalled from the preliminary reading, but it would be a very different matter to recall the detail of an episode's presentation, and combine versions independently and evenly.[26]

What we have just described seems, at least initially, consistent with Goulder's picture of Luke. However, a few problems arise upon a closer analysis of the passages where Luke is evidently relying both on the

---

22. Ibid., 179.
23. Ibid., 181.
24. Ibid.
25. Ibid., 180–81.
26. C. B. R. Pelling, "Plutarch's Method of Work in the Roman Lives," *Journal of Hellenic Studies* 99 (1979): 92.

Table 2
Sources for Luke 13:22–35 (Condemnation of Israel)
(Goulder, *LNP* 571–81; English translation from NRSV)

Luke 13:22–35	Visual Contact with Matthew	Matthean Texts by Reminiscence
22Jesus went through one town and village after another, teaching as he made his way to Jerusalem. [thematic link with Matt 9:35]		9:35: Then Jesus went about all the cities and villages, teaching in their synagogues, and proclaiming the good news of the kingdom, and curing every disease and every sickness.
23Someone asked him, Lord, will only a few be saved? He said to them, 24Strive to enter through the narrow door; for many, I tell you, will try to enter and will not be able. 25When once the owner of the house has got up and shut the door, and you begin to stand outside and to knock at the door, saying, Lord, open to us, then in reply he will say to you, I do not know where you come from. 26Then you will begin to say, We ate and drank with you, and you taught in our streets. 27But he will say, I do not know where you come from; go away from me, all you evildoers!	25:10–12: And while they went to buy it, the bridegroom came, and those who were ready went with him into the wedding banquet; and the door was shut. Later the other bridesmaids came also, saying, Lord, lord, open to us. But he replied, Truly I tell you, I do not know you.	7:13–14: Enter through the narrow gate; for the gate is wide and the road is easy that leads to destruction, and there are many who take it. For the gate is narrow and the road is hard that leads to life, and there are few who find it. 7:22–23: On that day many will say to me, Lord, Lord, did we not prophesy in your name, and cast out demons in your name, and do many deeds of power in your name? Then I will declare to them, I never knew you; go away from me, you evildoers. 24:43: But understand this: if the owner of the house [cf. Luke 13:25] had known in what part of the night the thief was coming, he would have stayed awake and would not have let his house be broken into.

text of Matthew visibly accessible and other portions of Matthew from memory. In Luke 13:22–18:8, several occasions where Luke's connection with Matthew is strongest in the texts are evidently being recalled from memory. In Luke 13:22–35 ("The Condemnation of Israel"), for example, Goulder imagines Luke beginning to work through his scroll

Table 2 (continued)
Sources for Luke 13:22–35 (Condemnation of Israel)
(Goulder, *LNP* 571–81; English translation from NRSV)

Luke 13:22–35	Visual Contact with Matthew	Matthean Texts by Reminiscence
[28]There will be weeping and gnashing of teeth when you see Abraham and Isaac and Jacob and all the prophets in the kingdom of God, and you yourselves thrown out. [29]Then people will come from east and west, from north and south, and will eat in the kingdom of God. [30]Indeed, some are last who will be first, and some are first who will be last.		8:11–12: I tell you, many will come from east and west and will eat with Abraham and Isaac and Jacob in the kingdom of heaven, while the heirs of the kingdom will be thrown into the outer darkness, where there will be weeping and gnashing of teeth. 20:16: So the last will be first, and the first will be last.
[31]At that very hour some Pharisees came and said to him, Get away from here, for Herod wants to kill you. [32]He said to them, Go and tell that fox for me, Listen, I am casting out demons and performing cures today and tomorrow, and on the third day I finish my work. [33]Yet today, tomorrow, and the next day I must be on my way, because it is impossible for a prophet to be killed outside of Jerusalem.	26:1–2: When Jesus had finished saying all these things, he said to his disciples, You know that after two days the Passover is coming, and the Son of Man will be handed over to be crucified.	14:1–14: At that time Herod the ruler heard reports about Jesus; and he said to his servants, This is John the Baptist.... Though Herod wanted to put him to death, he feared the crowd....His disciples came and...they went and told Jesus. Now when Jesus heard this, he withdrew from there.... When he went ashore, he saw a great crowd; and he had compassion for them and cured their sick.
[34]Jerusalem, Jerusalem, the city that kills the prophets and stones those who are sent to it! How often have I desired to gather your children together as a hen gathers her brood under her wings, and you were not willing! [35]See, your house is left to you. And I tell you, you will not see me until the time comes when you say, Blessed is the one who comes in the name of the Lord.	23:37–39: Jerusalem, Jerusalem, the city that kills the prophets and stones those who are sent to it! How often have I desired to gather your children together as a hen gathers her brood under her wings, and you were not willing! See, your house is left to you, desolate. For I tell you, you will not see me again until you say, Blessed is the one who comes in the name of the Lord.

of Matthew in reverse, having visual contact with Matt 23–26 (table 2). Clearly at Luke 13:34–35 ("The Lament over Jerusalem"), on Goulder's theory Luke has a clear visual contact with Matt 23:37–39 given the extensive verbatim agreement between the two. However, the contact seems almost as strong at Luke 13:28–30, where Luke evidently is working from memory with Matt 8:11–12 and 20:16. Here, the verbal similarities are quite strong, considerably stronger than where Luke is relying on the text visually "in front of him" (i.e., Matt 25:10–12).

A similar phenomenon exists at Luke 17:20–18:8 (table 3, pp. 76–77). Here, Goulder states that his theory provides an explanation for the presence of two verses not in Matt 24, specifically the introductory statement in Luke 17:20 and the saying on losing one's life in 17:33. At 17:20, Luke visually "borrows" from Matt 16:1–2 the motif of the Pharisees' questioning of Jesus and Jesus' subsequent answer (*LNP* 649). At Luke 17:25, Goulder argues that the presence of the phrase *great suffering* and the preposition *apo* constitute "a sure sign of the presence of Matthew 16[:21] on Luke's table as he writes" (*LNP* 652).[27] At Luke 17:33, Luke "borrows" from the text in front of him — Matt 16:25 — the saying on saving and losing one's life (*LNP* 654).[28] For it is the visual presence of Matt 16 on Luke's table that causes Luke to track its sequence and "not follow exactly the (excellent) order of Matthew 24 because Luke is drawing on Matthew 24 only secondarily" (*LNP* 649). Yet when one observes the parallels between Luke 17:20–18:8 with Matt 16 and 24, the data seems to suggest that, of the two choices, it is Matt 24 that Luke has "in front of him," as opposed to Matt 16, given the rather strong parallels between Luke 17 and Matt 24 throughout Luke 17, both in terms of general order and wording. If memory is at work here with Luke, it appears that Matt 16, not Matt 24, is drawn upon secondarily. Goulder himself, perhaps unconsciously, seems to "lapse" into thinking that Matt 24 is open in front of Luke when he describes Luke's *copying* of "the Matthean version [of Matt 24:37–39] almost verbatim" at Luke 17:26–27, a place where Goulder otherwise describes Luke's use of Matthew from memory (*LNP* 652).

Thus, in terms of the use of memory, Goulder's Luke, when "remembering" the Matthean text that is not "in front of him," is often closer

---

27. Goulder continues (*LNP* 652): " 'This generation' is an abbreviation for the elders, etc., who feature in other forms of the saying; it is likely to stem from the 'wicked and adulterous generation' which we have already noted from Mt. 16:4."

28. Interestingly, Goulder makes no mention of Matt 10:39, which provides an equally strong verbal parallel to Luke 17:33.

to the wording of that text from memory then the Matthean text open on his table.

As an alternative to both Goulder's theory and the Two-Source theory, the Neo-Griesbach or Two-Gospel hypothesis becomes implausible when one observes the self-described "pattern of alternating agreements" in Mark's Gospel, where Mark zigzags between his two sources, Matthew and Luke.[29] In my continuing work on the Synoptic Problem, I have found the habitual pattern of moving from one source to another regularly within individual pericopes difficult to imagine in light of the tendency of ancient authors to prefer to follow one source at a time, perhaps for mechanical reasons of working with scrolls and without the benefit of a writing table. While Goulder is clearly not imaging a scenario for Luke and his two sources exactly like that of Mark on the Two-Gospel hypothesis, Goulder does describe for Luke an "alternating pattern of agreement" of sorts: Luke regularly and habitually will move from one source to another, that is, from his text with which he has visual contact to texts "stored" in his memory. While Goulder is technically correct in arguing that his Luke "follows one source at a time," functionally, Luke repeatedly jumps between two "sources" — the "base-of-the-moment" (i.e., the text physically and visually "in front of him") and the treasury of texts in his memory (Goulder, "Crank," 113).[30] Thus, while Goulder's simple description of "one source at a time" does, in fact, sound "simple" and is consistent with the general practice of ancient writers, it is in reality a more complicated procedure of regularly moving back and forth between the physically present visual text to text "stored" in memory within individual pericopes, often just for brief phrases or words.

What about Luke's movement through Matt 16–25? Is Luke's use of Matthew in this section backward in movement? Goulder's table of selected parallels does seem to support this assertion. However, when one looks at all of the episodes in Luke 13:22–18:8, along with their

---

29. W. R. Farmer describes this as "a pattern of alternation in wording, where Mark agrees closely now with one of his sources and then suddenly just as closely with the other"; *The Synoptic Problem* (New York: Macmillan, 1964; repr. Dillsboro: Western North Carolina Press, 1976), 241.

30. In response to Downing, Goulder describes Luke's technique as follows ("Luke's Compositional Options," 151): "One Gospel at a time, reminiscences from the other, no attempt at word-for-word reproduction where the sources agree, the importation of the author's own interpretations or those familiar to him."

Table 3
Sources for Luke 17:20–18:8 (Coming of the Son of Man)
(Goulder, *LNP* 648–64; English translation from NRSV)

Luke 17:20–18:8	Visual Contact with Matthew 16	Matthean Texts by Reminiscence (Matthew 24)
20Once Jesus was asked by the Pharisees when the kingdom of God was coming, and he answered [them], The kingdom of God is not coming with things that can be observed;	1The Pharisees and Sadducees came, and to test Jesus they asked him to show them a sign from heaven. 2He answered them, When it is evening, you say, It will be fair weather, for the sky is red. 3And in the morning, It will be stormy today, for the sky is red and threatening. You know how to interpret the appearance of the sky, but you cannot interpret the signs of the times. 4An evil and adulterous generation asks for a sign, but no sign will be given to it except the sign of Jonah. Then he left them and went away.	
21nor will they say, Look, here it is! or There it is! For, in fact, the kingdom of God is among you. 22Then he said to the disciples, The days are coming when you will long to see one of the days of the Son of Man, and you will not see it. 23They will say to you, Look there! or Look here! Do not go, do not set off in pursuit. 24For as the lightning flashes and lights up the sky from one side to the other, so will the Son of Man be in his day. 25But first he must endure much suffering and be rejected by this generation. 26Just as it was in the days of Noah, so too it will be in the days of the Son of Man. 27They were eating and drinking, and marrying and being given in marriage, until the day Noah entered the ark, and the flood came and destroyed all of them. 28Likewise, just as it was in the days of Lot: they were eating and drinking, buying and selling, planting and building, 29but on the day that Lot left Sodom, it rained fire and sulfur from heaven and destroyed all of them 30 — it will be like that on the day that the Son of Man is revealed.	28Truly I tell you, there are some standing here who will not taste death before they see the Son of Man coming [cf. Luke 18:8] in his kingdom. 21From that time on, Jesus began to show his disciples that he must go to Jerusalem and undergo great suffering at the hands of the elders and chief priests and scribes, and be killed, and on the third day be raised. 22And Peter took him aside and began to rebuke him, saying, God forbid it, Lord! This must never happen to you. 23But he turned and said to Peter, Get behind me, Satan! You are a stumbling block to me; for you are setting your mind not on divine things but on human things. 24Then Jesus told his disciples, If any want to become my followers, let them deny themselves and take up their cross and follow me.	23Then if anyone says to you, Look! Here is the Messiah! or There he is! — do not believe it. 24For false messiahs and false prophets will appear and produce great signs and omens, to lead astray, if possible, even the elect. 26So, if they say to you, Look! He is in the wilderness, do not go out. If they say, Look! He is in the inner rooms, do not believe it. 27For as the lightning comes from the east and flashes as far as the west, so will be the coming of the Son of Man. 28Wherever the corpse is, there the vultures will gather. 37For as the days of Noah were, so will be the coming of the Son of Man. 38For as in those days before the flood they were eating and drinking, marrying and giving in marriage, until the day Noah entered the ark, 39and they knew nothing until the flood came and swept them all away, so too will be the coming of the Son of Man. 40Then two will be in the field; one will be taken and one will be left.

Table 3 (continued)
Sources for Luke 17:20–18:8 (Coming of the Son of Man)
(Goulder, *LNP* 648–64; English translation from NRSV)

Luke 17:20–18:8	Visual Contact with Matthew 16	Matthean Texts by Reminiscence (Matthew 24)
[31]On that day, anyone on the housetop who has belongings in the house must not come down to take them away; and likewise anyone in the field must not turn back. [32]Remember Lot's wife.		[17]The one on the housetop must not go down to take what is in the house; [18]the one in the field must not turn back to get a coat.
[33]Those who try to make their life secure will lose it, but those who lose their life will keep it. [34]I tell you, on that night there will be two in one bed; one will be taken and the other left. [35]There will be two women grinding meal together; one will be taken and the other left. [37]Then they asked him, Where, Lord? He said to them, Where the corpse is, there the vultures will gather.	[25]For those who want to save their life will lose it, and those who lose their life for my sake will find it. [26]For what will it profit them if they gain the whole world but forfeit their life? Or what will they give in return for their life?	[40]Then two will be in the field; one will be taken and one will be left. [41]Two women will be grinding meal together; one will be taken and one will be left.
[18:1]Then Jesus told them a parable about their need to pray always and not to lose heart. [2]He said, In a certain city there was a judge who neither feared God nor had respect for people. [3]In that city there was a widow who kept coming to him and saying, Grant me justice against my opponent. [4]For a while he refused; but later he said to himself, Though I have no fear of God and no respect for anyone, [5]yet because this widow keeps bothering me, I will grant her justice, so that she may not wear me out by continually coming. [6]And the Lord said, Listen to what the unjust judge says. [7]And will not God grant justice to his chosen ones who cry to him day and night? Will he delay long in helping them? [8]I tell you, he will quickly grant justice to them. And yet, when the Son of Man comes, will he find faith on earth?		[28]Wherever the corpse is, there the vultures will gather.
	[27]For the Son of Man is to come with his angels in the glory of his Father, and then he will repay everyone for what has been done. [28]Truly I tell you, there are some standing here who will not taste death before they see the Son of Man coming [cf. Luke 17:22] in his kingdom.	[44]Therefore you also must be ready, for the Son of Man is coming at an unexpected hour. [45]Who then is the faithful and wise slave, whom his master has put in charge of his household, to give the other slaves their allowance of food at the proper time? [46]Blessed is that slave whom his master will find at work when he arrives.

Matthean (and Markan) parallels, the sequence is not as unidirectional as Goulder would like to imagine. Table 1 illustrates Luke moving both backward and forward, often within individual episodes. In addition, on at least two occasions, Luke appears to follow the Markan wording in particular pericopes: the parable of the salt[31] and possibly the divorce statement.[32] Even if Goulder's Luke is recalling these sections "by reminiscence" it makes a scenario, originally seeming to be rather simple, become quite complicated.

It is also worth pointing out the places where Luke is not consistently moving backward through Matt 16–25, despite Goulder's general description to the contrary. For example, Goulder argues that the main inspiration for Luke's parables of the unjust steward (Luke 16:1–13) and the rich man and Lazarus (16:14–31) comes from Matt 18:23–25, the parable of the unmerciful servant, the text open to Luke at that point as he works in reverse through Matthew's scroll. However, Goulder also states that Luke, in his writing of the rich man and Lazarus parable, is also inspired by his "eye . . . fall[ing] on" Jesus' statement about the easier time a camel would have going through an eye of a needle than a "rich man" would have entering the kingdom of heaven (19:24). Thus there appears to be some *forward* turning in Matthew's scroll as Luke is working through the scroll in reverse.[33]

In addition, by the time Luke gets to writing 13:22–18:8, where he is working through Matt 16–25 in reverse, he already had some visual contact with that section from Matthew. For example, the Lucan woes (Luke 11:37–54) were written by Luke's having visual contact with Matthew's woes in chapter 23.[34] Likewise, at Luke's statements on watchfulness and faithfulness (Luke 12:35–48), Luke has "advance" visual contact

---

31. Luke 14:34–35 || Matt 5:13; *kalon oun to halas* comes from Mark 9:50.

32. Luke 16:18 || Matt 19:9; the lack of an unchastity exception clause and the statement regarding women and divorce may come from Mark 10:11–12.

33. C. M. Tuckett notices this as well: "This seems both difficult to envisage in itself and also contradictory of Luke's alleged general policy. Luke is meant to be working backward, not forward, through Matthew, and also ignoring Matthew's treatment of Markan material. Yet Goulder's theory suggests that Luke's eye was caught by a saying 24 verses ahead of the point in Matthew he has reached (and 24 verses is not just one line!)"; see "The Existence of Q," in *The Gospel behind the Gospels: Current Studies on Q* (ed. R. A. Piper; Novum Testamentum Supplement 75; Leiden: Brill, 1995), 44.

34. For example, Goulder states that at Luke 11:43 Luke has "the Matthean version in front of him at [Matt] 23:6f." (*LNP* 521).

with Matt 24. For the first part of this pericope, Luke has Matt 16 open in front of him; Luke uses Matt 24:43–44 as he writes Luke 12:39–40. However, at 12:42, Luke turns to Matt 24, and through direct visual contact uses Matt 24:45–51 as he writes Luke 12:42–51.[35] Thus, perhaps Goulder's picture of Luke should be modified to account for Luke's visual contact with sections of Matt 16–25 prior to its reverse contextualization at Luke 13:22–18:8, as well as accounting for Luke's occasional deviation from the unidirectional movement in reverse through Matt 16–25.

Ancient Media and Luke's "Backward" Contextualization of Matthew

Goulder is convinced that Luke's backward movement is "psychologically believable." But is it technically feasible? It would be difficult enough working consistently backward through a scroll of Matthew, given that scrolls were designed for start-to-finish reading (not necessarily in one sitting), offering the reader sequential access forward (as opposed to random and reverse!).

As is well established, the predominant medium used by writers in the first century C.E. was the scroll or book-roll.[36] According to Harry Gamble, papyrus or parchment scrolls could conceivably be of any length, but were 3.5 meters on average.[37] Callimachus (ca. 310/305–ca. 240 B.C.E.) once argued, "A big book [is] a big nuisance" (*mega biblion kakon*).[38] Therefore, the greatest literary "nuisances" of antiquity would have been Thucydides and Homer, whose works in scroll form would have mea-

---

35. *LNP* 549–51: "Luke (the text assures us) has at this point [i.e., Luke 12:40] had enough of retailing Matthew 24–25 from memory: he rolls the scroll on to the parable of the servant (Mt. 24:45–51), and 83 out of 102 words in the two versions are identical" (549).

36. Many references to this can be found in antiquity, including several in the New Testament. See, e.g., the uses of *biblion* in Matt 19:7; Mark 10:4; Luke 4:17 (twice), 20; John 20:30; 21:25; Gal 3:10; 2 Tim 4:13; Heb 9:19; 10:7; Rev 1:11; 5:1, 2, 3, 4, 5, 8, 9; 6:14; 10:8; 13:8; 17:8; 20:12 (thrice); 21:27; 22:7, 9, 10, 18 (twice), 19 (twice); and *biblos* in Matt 1:1; Mark 12:26; Luke 3:4; 20:42; Acts 1:20; 7:42; 19:19; Phil 4:3; Rev 3:5; 20:15.

37. H. Gamble, *Books and Readers in the Early Church* (New Haven: Yale University Press, 1995), 45.

38. Cited in D. Diringer, *The Hand-Produced Book* (London: Hutchinson's Scientific and Technical Publications, 1953), 132; B. M. Metzger, *The Text of the New Testament* (New York: Oxford University Press, 1992), 5 n. 2.

sured 300 feet and 150 feet, respectively.[39] Bruce Metzger estimates that
Luke's Gospel measured thirty-one or thirty-two feet as a papyrus scroll,
closer to the typical maximum length of thirty-five feet.[40] A book-roll or
scroll allowed the reader continuous or sequential access to a particular document, with its design most conducive to start-to-finish reading.
In addition, reading from a scroll, let alone writing on one, was quite
an operation that demanded great care and coordination.[41] And working with a scroll could be hazardous to one's health. The younger Pliny
(61/62–113 c.e.) relates the account of the elderly Verginius Rufus who
broke his hip while slipping during an attempt to "gather up" a scroll
that had fallen on a newly polished floor.[42]

Goulder is imagining Luke working backward through the sequence
of the scroll of Matthew at this point, but forward through each individual pericope. In attempting to answer the question whether this
is technically feasible, allow me to use an analogy from modern audio
media: Goulder's description of Luke at 13:22–18:8 is comparable to
recording the song sequence from an another cassette tape in reverse
onto a blank audio cassette tape, but recording each individual song
forward. This is a scenario that one could easily accomplish with a compact disk as the audio source, since a CD player can be programmed in
this fashion and offers the listener random access to the song selection.
It is an unnecessarily difficult task, however, to attempt this scenario

39. Cf. Diringer, *Hand-Produced Book*, 127–29.

40. Metzger, *Text of the New Testament*, 5–6.

41. L. Avrin, *Scribes, Script, and Books: The Book Arts from Antiquity to the Renaissance* (Chicago:
American Library Association, 1991), 153: "The ancient reader of Greek [scrolls] was inconvenienced
in several ways. Holding the scroll open as one read and simultaneously rerolling the scroll in one's
left hand, required exceptional coordination. Looking up an exact quotation in a different scroll was
totally discouraging. If the scroll fell to the floor, retrieving it was a nuisance, much worse if it ripped.
Unless the reader was familiar with the text, the absence of word spacing and punctuation slowed
comprehension. When the reader found the scroll with the end of the story first, he or she had to
reroll it before having the pleasure of reading the book. No wonder that when readers finished the
scroll, they [typically] did not rewind it for the next person!"

42. Pliny, *Letters* 2.1.5 (To Voconius Romanus): "He [Verginius Rufus] had reached the age of
eighty-three, living in close retirement and deeply respected by us all, and his health was good, apart
from a trembling of the hands, not enough to trouble him. Only death when it came was slow and
painful, though we can only admire the way he faced it. He was rehearsing the delivery of his address
of thanks to the Emperor [Nerva] for his election to his third consulship, when he had occasion to
take up a heavy book, the weight of which made it fall out of his hands, as he was an old man and
standing at the time. He bent down to pick [*colligitque*; lit., 'gather'] it up, and lost his footing on the
slippery polished floor, so that he fell and fractured his hip. This was so badly set, and because of his
age it never mended properly."

with two audiocassette tapes — one as the source tape and the other as the recording tape. All in all, it is a tremendously difficult scenario to imagine (its purpose is equally difficult to imagine). As far as I can tell, Goulder provides no convincing explanation as to why Luke is working backward rather than forward. If, as Goulder himself states, the sequence of Matthew's teaching material for Luke is not as important as Mark's narrative material, why not just roll the scroll back to Matt 16 and work from there following the scroll's sequence? Luke, instead, opts for the more technically difficult procedure of working through Matthew in reverse, a procedure that would appear to be quite peculiar in the ancient literary world. In fact, it is a technique that is very different from Luke's other movement "through Matthew 1–12 and 23–25 . . . carefully and in order" (Goulder, "Crank," 121), as well as Luke's rather consistent use of Mark in sequence.[43] The pericope that precedes this section in Luke (13:22–18:8) is the parable of the mustard seed and leaven (13:18–21). Goulder argues (*LNP* 566) that here Luke "opts for the Matthean version" (Matt 13:31–33). Instead of moving on to the next pericopes in the Matthean sequence (the kingdom parables of Matt 13), Luke advances his Matthew scroll to Matt 25, and from that point works backward through Matthew's scroll to Matt 16.[44] Given the above discussion, it seems that this sort of procedure is somewhat implausible, particularly given the limitations of scroll design.

Most codicologists argue that the codex did not come into regular use until the late second century at the earliest. We do, however, find primitive literary ancestors in the form of wax tablets and notebooks in the first century. Goulder rightly imagines that Matthew's Gospel was composed and originally circulated as a scroll. What about Matthew in

---

43. *Pace* Tuckett ("Existence of Q," 44–45): "[Goulder's] discussion of Luke's order still provides no very convincing explanation for why Luke should have selected and divided up the material in Matthew in the way he must have done if he knew it in its Matthean form and order. When one couples this with Luke's very conservative treatment of the order of Mark, the problem becomes even more acute. Why should Luke have had so much respect for the order of Mark, scarcely changing it at all, and yet change the order of Matthew at almost every point? Streeter's comment that such a procedure seems like that of a 'crank,' although expressed somewhat polemically, still has force. Not even Goulder's defence of the 'order of a crank' seems sufficient to meet this problem"; cf. also Tuckett, *Q and the History of Early Christianity* [Edinburgh: T&T Clark, 1996], 30–31).

44. It should be noted that in Luke 13:22–30 Goulder has Luke moving not just simply backward from Matt 25 onward, but moving between Matt 9:35; 25:10–12; 7:13–14; 7:22–23; 25:41; 8:11–12; 19:30. See Goulder, *LNP* 570–75.

(early) codex form? Does this medium help Goulder's case at all? Again, the modern analogy of the compact disk allows one to imagine Goulder's procedure differently. Goulder's picture of Luke would become more be-lievable if he imagined Luke's copy of Matthew (and Mark, but less so) was in some sort of early codex format. This would allow Luke ran-dom access to Matthew, which is the implicit procedure that Luke often follows with Matthew on Goulder's theory. However, the scroll had the advantage over its literary counterpart, the codex, in allowing the reader to control to a certain degree how much of the text could be displayed.[45] "With a codex," Small states, "you are locked into what is on the obverse and reverse of each page."[46] If the Matthean pericopes in Luke's exem-plars were overly long, then the scroll theory could have more currency than the codex. But Matt 22:1–10 appears to be the longest section of text that Luke is adapting (Luke 14:15–24) in 13:22–18:8. Thus, a codex prototype could be imagined as the medium for Luke's Matthew. Goulder does not, of course, imagine codices but scrolls.[47]

Conclusion

With sincere respect and appreciation, I offer some concluding remarks. I think that there are several problems with the procedure Goulder de-scribes. First, the conception of Luke's use of a writing table needs to be reevaluated. Assuming that the literary and artistic evidence is both accurate and representative, we should conclude that likely none of the evangelists had access to a writing table. This is a relatively minor point of contention, since most Synoptic source critics are equally guilty of presupposing writing tables for the Synoptic evangelists. Whatever source-critical solution one assumes, one is not exempt from having to explain realistically how a later author brings together two sources without the aid of a writing table, be it Matthew and Luke on the Neo-

---

45. See T. C. Skeat, "Roll Versus Codex — A New Approach?" *Zeitschrift für Papyrologie und Epigraphik* 8 (1990): 263–68.

46. Small, *Wax Tablets of the Mind*, 155.

47. *Contra* Downing, "Paradigm Perplex," 18: While the codex is the "easier path" for Goulder's Luke, he is "firmly confined to scrolls."

Griesbach theory, Mark and Q on the Two-Source theory, or Matthew and Mark on Goulder's hypothesis.

Second, the notion that Luke works systematically and consistently through Matt 16–25 in reverse needs to be rethought. There are places where Luke appears to have visual contact with other sections from Matthew, as opposed to contact through memory. But this backward movement is not consistently followed, since Luke on occasion moves forward in his exemplar, then back again.

Third, the use of scrolls (particularly without the aid of a writing desk) placed severe restrictions on what exactly Luke could accomplish. Operating a scroll in reverse strikes me as both peculiar (and potentially anachronistic) and unnecessarily difficult in a technical sense. If Luke were free to resequence the sayings material in Matthew, why would he choose such an odd method, that is, the systematic reverse contextualization of Matt 16–25? I think Goulder would be better served describing a nonsystematic, nonsequential use of Matthew at Luke 13:22–18:8, one where Luke is free to move in his scroll where and when he pleases in order to incorporate Matthew's material prior to the passion narrative. If this is the case, however, then Luke does, in fact, look a bit like a crank, no matter how polemical and dated Streeter's description is.

Goulder's contribution to Synoptic Problem discussion is clearly significant and should not be underestimated. Goulder's work continues to be characterized by boldness and alacrity, never hesitating to take on the consensus in Synoptic scholarship. I offer my remarks as a challenge given with the utmost respect and sincere thanks for Michael Goulder's ongoing contribution to Gospels study, a contribution that has certainly enhanced my own work, making it as equally enjoyable as it is challenging.

FROM ESCHATOLOGY
TO IMPERIALISM

Mapping the Territory of Acts 2

Gary Gilbert

According to the Acts of the Apostles, after Jesus had ascended into heaven and Matthias had been identified as the appropriate replacement for Judas, the apostles and others who believed in Jesus as the Messiah gathered in Jerusalem during the celebration of the Jewish Festival of Shavuot, referred to in Acts as Pentecost. Suddenly a thunderous sound and a fiery apparition appeared before them. Empowered by the Holy Spirit, each began to speak in other languages. Jews from throughout the Diaspora now dwelling in Jerusalem witnessed this event and were astounded that they heard the apostles speaking in the native language of each. As if to underscore the linguistic diversity present in the crowd, the Jewish speakers named the regions from which they had come: Parthia, Media, Elam, Mesopotamia, Judea, Cappadocia, Pontus, Asia, Phrygia, Pamphylia, Egypt, parts of Libya belonging to Cyrene, Rome, Crete, and Arabia. In typical Lucan fashion, the event created a division among the audience:[1] some wanted to learn more, whereas others sneered and attributed the babbling behavior to drunkenness.

The brief passage in Acts 2:1–13 and particularly the list of nations

---

1. Scenes in which crowds divide over the appearance or speeches of major characters include 4:1–4 (Peter's speech); 5:12–21 (response to signs and wonders); 5:27–39 (apostles before the Sanhedrin); 13:42–52 (Paul and Barnabas in Pisidian Antioch); 14:1–7 (Paul and Barnabas in Iconium); 17:4–5 (Paul and Silas in Thessalonica); 17:32–34 (Paul in Athens); 18:5–8 (Paul in Corinth); 23:9–10 (Paul before the Sanhedrin); 28:24 (Paul in Rome). A more detailed analysis of this passage, including a discussion of alternate theories, can be found in G. Gilbert, "The List of Nations in Acts 2: Roman Propaganda and the Lucan Response," *Journal of Biblical Literature* (forthcoming).

presents scholars with no shortage of difficulties. What objective visual and audible events are being described? Does the story tell of the disciples engaged in ecstatic speech (i.e., speaking in tongues) or using recognizable languages?[2] The reading Judea is beset with textual difficulties and seems out of place. Why would Jews marvel at being able to understand Galilean disciples?[3] Either in recognition of this difficulty or to provide a more original reading, early Christian writers supplied alterative geographical locations.[4] Tertullian and Augustine present the reading Armenia, while Jerome inserts Syria, and John Chrysostom offers India. This pericope involves redactional difficulties as well. Why did the author of Acts arrange the list in this particular order? The list moves generally from east to west, but at the very end doubles back and concludes in the east with Arabia. Are Crete and Arabia later scribal additions to the list?[5] Why mention Media and Elam, regions that no longer existed in a political sense when Acts was written? Finally, there is a question of sources. Did Luke compose the list of nations himself or does the list's origin reside elsewhere?

The issue of sources for New Testament documents is a subject near and dear to Michael Goulder. Goulder's career has been marked by conviction, passion, and imagination to reconstruct the history of the literary development of the Gospels. His search for the sources behind the Gospels has led him to propound the lectionary hypothesis and to develop his very meticulous and unflagging support of the FGH.[6] The latter posits a relationship among the Synoptic Gospels that preserves Markan priority

2. The use of the term *dialektos* in 2:6 weighs heavily in favor of the crowd hearing recognizable languages. See E. Haenchen, *The Acts of the Apostles* (Philadelphia: Westminster, 1971), 168. The mention of "tongues" (*glōssai*) and the concluding comment that some thought the disciples were drunk, however, suggest the incomprehensible vocalizing characteristic of ecstatic speech and should be compared with similar descriptions in Paul (e.g., 1 Cor 14:18). See the review in G. Schneider, *Die Apostelgeschichte* (Freiburg: Herder, 1980), 243–45.

3. It is unlikely that this reference has anything to do with distinctive Galilean dialects. See F. F. Bruce, *The Acts of the Apostles* (Grand Rapids: Eerdmans, 1951), 84.

4. On the textual problems, see E. Gütting, "Der geographische Horizont der sogenannten Völkerlist des Lukas (Acta 2.9–11)," *Zeitschrift für neutestamentliche Wissenschaft* 66 (1975): 149–69; although I do not agree with his conclusion that *ioudaian* was originally *lykian*. It should be noted that the manuscripts and versions agree on the reading Judea.

5. Earlier versions of the list may have ended with Rome, the city where the dramatic climax of Acts takes place. Suggested by Haenchen, *Acts*, 171 n. 1.

6. Among the many of works of M. D. Goulder in this area, the following should be noted: *THA*; *MLM*; *LNP*; "The Pre-Marcan-Gospel," *Scottish Journal of Theology* 47 (1994): 453–71. For a detailed examination of Goulder's work, see Mark S. Goodacre, *Goulder and the Gospels: An Examination of*

but dispenses with Q. Rather, the theory argues, Mark's Gospel became a source for the writing of Matthew. In turn, Luke composed his account of Jesus' life and death using both Mark and Matthew. The theory obviates the need to reconstruct a Q document. The material common to Matthew and Luke arises from the latter having copied from the former. Moreover, the theory explains the existence of minor agreements, instances where Matthew and Luke agree against Mark and are clearly not a part of any version of Q (e.g., Matt 26:68; Luke 22:64). As a way of honoring Goulder, I wish to take up the issue of sources, but focus on the Book of Acts. I will explore the possible sources or inspiration for the list of nations in Acts 2 and the implications this analysis has for our understanding of Acts and Lucan theology. In anticipation of the ensuing discussion, I hope to show that the list of nations presents an ironic reading of similar lists that became a standard form of propaganda used to glorify and legitimate Rome's claim to universal dominion. Although Acts uses this well-known rhetorical tool, it constructs a very different, indeed competing, imperial system. For Acts, the empire truly belongs not to Caesar, but to Jesus who as Lord and Savior reigns over all people.

To begin, we should place the verses under examination within their narrative context. The book of Acts begins with Jesus' final preascension commission to his apostles: they are to be his witnesses to the end of the earth (Acts 1:8). Once the ranks of the apostles have been replenished, with Matthias replacing the disgraced Judas, the author turns his attention to the event that marks the transition from the time of Jesus to the time of the church,[7] or as Goulder once referred to it, "the time for the initiation of the Church" (*THA* 149). About a week after Jesus ascended into heaven, the Festival of Pentecost arrived. Unexpectedly and suddenly, all the disciples who had gathered together were filled with the Holy Spirit and began to speak in foreign tongues. Also present at this event were pious Jews (*ioudaioi andres eulabeis*) from every nation under heaven (2:5). As the group broke into its linguistic display, the astonished observers wondered how these Galileans could each be

---

a New Paradigm (Journal for the Study of the New Testament Supplement 133; Sheffield: Sheffield Academic Press, 1996).

7. D. Juel, *Luke-Acts: The Promise of History* (Atlanta: John Knox, 1983), 57.

speaking in a language not their own. Peter addressed the crowd, stating
that they had witnessed no untoward event, but the fulfillment of biblical prophecy (2:16–21). He then launched into an extended discourse
on the death, resurrection, and enthronement of Jesus, supporting his
position with quotations from Joel 2, Ps 16, and Ps 110 (Acts 2:22–35).
He concluded by noting that the Jesus whom the Jews had crucified God
had made Lord and Messiah (2:36). The crowd grew concerned because
of Peter's speech and asked him what they should do. Peter summoned
them to repent and be baptized so that their sins may be forgiven and
that they may receive the Holy Spirit (2:37–39). The story concludes
with the notice that about three thousand persons were baptized and
became faithful members of the community (2:40–42).

According to Martin Dibelius, the pattern established in this scene —
major event followed by kerygmatic speech, including scriptural proof
and exhortation to repentance — is typical not only of Acts but also
of the preaching customs of the time.[8] The pattern commonly features
the presence of a crowd. In this scene the crowd serves three purposes.
It functions as the narrative audience for Peter's speech, the source of
the three thousand new believers, and as a witness to the event itself.
The crowd confirms that the bestowal of the Holy Spirit was not a
private affair meant for and known only by the faithful. Rather, this new
period, inaugurated by the presence of the Holy Spirit, began with a very
public event.

The crowd does not consist of a random collection of people. The
author specifically identifies them as pious people, Jews originally from
the Diaspora and now living in Jerusalem. The list of nations that follows
provides further specificity to the generic claim that Jews from "every
nation under heaven" were living in Jerusalem. By emphasizing that
Jews from throughout the world had come to live in Jerusalem, Acts
may have wished to invoke the eschatological expectations of biblical
prophets and later Jewish writers. Isaiah, for instance, speaks of what
will happen on the day of the Lord:

---

8. M. Dibelius, *Studies in Acts of the Apostles* (New York: Scribner, 1956), 165.

At this time, God's hand will recover the remnant that is left of
his people, from Assyria, from Egypt, from Pathros, from Ethiopia,
from Elam, and Shinar, from Hamath, and from the coastlands of
the sea. He will raise a signal for the nations, and will assemble the
outcasts of Israel, and gather the dispersed of Judah from the four
corners of the earth. (Isa 11:11–12)

Throughout the Second Temple period, Jewish writers expressed a vision similar to that of Isaiah's in which the ingathering of the Jewish
exiles would constitute a major event in the eschatological or messianic
period. First Enoch includes the gathering of the dispersed as one of the
incidents described in the animal apocalypse (1 Enoch 90:33). Correspondence found in 2 Maccabees ostensibly from the Jews in Jerusalem
and Judea and Judas to Aristobulus and the Jews in Egypt encourages
the recipients to celebrate the purification of the temple on Kislev 25
(i.e., Hanukkah). The letter concludes with an expression of hope that
"God will gather us from everywhere under heaven into his holy place"
(2 Macc 2:18). In the famous Psalm of Solomon 17, the author, drawing
on Isa 66:20, envisions the time when the children of Israel will be returned to the land by the nations that drove them out (Ps. Sol. 17:31).
A hymn of praise, possibly written in the second century B.C.E. and later
included in some versions of the Wisdom of Ben Sira, expresses thanks
to God who "gathers the dispersed of Israel."[9] According to 2 Esdras
(= 4 Ezra), God's agent, variously identified as the man coming on the
clouds (2 Esd 13:3) and the Son of God (13:37), will gather to himself
the ten tribes that had been led into captivity (13:39–40). The work
known as 2 Baruch offers a similar vision in its description of the future
assembling of those who had been dispersed (2 Bar 78:7). The theme
of a future gathering of exiles appears frequently in rabbinic literature
(Babylonian Talmud, tractate Berakhot 12b; tractate Pesahim 88a; tractate Sanhedrin 110b; Jerusalem Talmud, tractate Berakhot 2:4, 4d; Esther
Rabbah 1:8) and finds its liturgical expression in the tenth benediction in

---

9. The hymn is found in a medieval manuscript discovered in the Cairo Geniza, but not in any
ancient version (Hebrew, Greek, or Syriac); P. W. Skehan and A. A. Di Lella, The Wisdom of Ben Sira
(Anchor Bible 39; New York: Doubleday, 1987), 568–71.

the *Shemoneh Esreh,* possibly codified by the nascent rabbinic community in the late first or early second century (Mishnah, tractate *Berakhot* 4:3; Tosefta, tractate *Berakhot* 3:13, 25; Babylonian Talmud, tractate *Berakhot* 28b; tractate *Megillah* 17b).[10]

Several modern commentaries adopt the vision of eschatological ingathering in their interpretations of the Pentecost episode and the list of nations in Acts 2. Donald Juel speaks of the list as the fulfillment of prophecies about the restoration of the scattered people of Israel.[11] Luke Johnson describes the event at Pentecost as the restoration of the remnant people: "[The story of Pentecost tells of] the first fulfilment of the promise [in which] Jews from the diaspora are included. . . . Just as the twelve represent the nucleus of the people that is being restored, so does this audience represent all the lands to which the Jews have been dispersed."[12] Jacob Jervell refers to the list of nations as a representation of the Jewish Diaspora.[13] A final example comes from the commentary of Gerhard Krodel, who views the "presence of these Jews from every nation under heaven [to symbolize] the beginning of the gathering of the scattered tribes of Israel and thus the restoration of the kingdom to Israel before the parousia."[14] While absent a consensus, the interpretation that the list of nations is related to and draws on Jewish eschatological prophecy has become common among contemporary scholars.

Turning our attention from some of the more recent interpreters of Acts to one of the most ancient, we encounter a striking difference in the way the list of nations has been understood. Early in the third century, Tertullian wrote a treatise entitled *Against the Jews,* which tells of an ostensible debate between a Christian and a Jewish proselyte. In the opening sections, the Christian expounds upon the idea that:

---

10. On the dating and early history of the *Shemoneh Esreh,* also known as the *Tefillah* or *Amidah,* see I. Elbogen, *Jewish Liturgy* (trans. R. Scheindlin; Philadelphia: Jewish Publication Society; New York: Jewish Theological Seminary, 1993), 25–37; 201–3; and, J. Heinemann, *Prayer in the Talmud* (Studia Judaica 9; Berlin: de Gruyter, 1977), 23–29, 45–50.

11. Juel, *Luke-Acts,* 58.

12. L. T. Johnson, *The Acts of the Apostles* (Sacra Pagina 5; Collegeville, Minn.: Liturgical, 1992), 45, 47.

13. J. Jervell, *Die Apostelgeschichte* (Göttingen: Vandenhoeck & Ruprecht, 1998), 1.136.

14. G. Krodel, *Acts* (Augsburg Commentary; Minneapolis: Augsburg, 1986), 77.

since Israel has departed from the Lord and rejected his grace, the Old Testament no longer has any force but must be interpreted spiritually.... The code of the Jews, written on tablets of stone, came immeasurably after that which was unwritten, the law of nature. Consequently, the former is not necessary for salvation; circumcision, observance of the Sabbath, the ancient sacrifices have been abolished [and] replaced by the priest of the new sacrifice [and] observer of the eternal Sabbath.[15]

In chapter 7, Tertullian has the Christian inquire rhetorically of his Jewish interlocutor whether Jesus is the Messiah about whom the prophets have spoken or whether the Jews are correct in thinking that the Messiah is yet to come. Tertullian then proceeds to cite Isa 45:1, which he reads as follows:

Thus says the Lord God to my Christ the Lord [reading *kyrio* instead of *kyro*, the proper noun Cyrus, King of Persia], whose right hand I have held, that the nations may hear him: the powers of kings will I burst asunder; I will open before him the gates, and the cities shall not be closed to him.

These things, Tertullian continues, have now been fulfilled:

For upon whom else have the universal nations believed, but upon the Christ who is already come? For whom have the nations believed — Parthians, Medes, Elamites, and they who inhabit Mesopotamia, Armenia, Phrygia, Cappadocia, and they who dwell in Pontus and Asia and Pamphylia, tarriers in Egypt, and the inhabitants of the region of Africa which is beyond Cyrene, Romans and proselytes, and, in Jerusalem, Jews, and all other nations.

To the geographic names Tertullian found in Acts 2, he adds

the Gaetulians and the manifold confines of the Moors, all the limits of the Spains and the diverse nations of the Gauls and the haunts of the Britons — inaccessible to the Romans, but subjugated

---

15. J. Quasten, *Patrology* (Westminster, Md.: Christian Classics, 1983 [orig. 1950]), 2.268–69.

to Christ — and of the Sarmatians and the Dacians and Germans and Scythians and of many remote nations and of provinces and islands many, to us unknown, and which we can scarce enumerate.

Tertullian then contrasts Jesus, who had received universal affirmation, with Solomon who reigned only in Judea; Darius who ruled over the Babylonians and Parthians; Nebuchadnezzar who held dominion from India unto Ethiopia; and the kingdoms and empires of Alexander of Macedon, the Germans, Britons, Moors, and even the Romans who were confined to their own regions. "But Christ's name is extending everywhere, believed everywhere, worshiped by all the above enumerated nations, reigning everywhere, adored everywhere, conferred equally everywhere upon all." For Tertullian the list of nations serves as proof for the fulfillment, not of the prophesied ingathering of Jews from the Diaspora, but of the entire world coming under the dominion of Christ.

At first glance, it seems that Tertullian has wrenched the list out of its narrative context. The list of nations in Acts 2 specifically identifies those named in the list as Jews living in Jerusalem and, therefore, presumably means to suggest the ingathering of Jewish exiles. Tertullian, however, uses these names and others for a different purpose. The list of nations validates Tertullian's argument that Jesus is the true ruler of the world. Rather than being a highly idiosyncratic interpretation, however, Tertullian's reading provides important insights into Acts 2 and, more generally, into the Lucan presentation of the expansion of Christianity.

Our exploration of the territory described in Acts sets out by revisiting the question of sources. Scholars almost universally agree that the author of Acts did not invent the list of nations. Beyond this general statement, however, they scramble to identify the precise source from which he drew this information. The commentaries are littered with various possibilities. We have already noticed one example. Isaiah envisions how the Lord "will recover the remnant that is left of his people." He then proceeds to list those places from which the "outcasts of Israel" and "dispersed of Judah" will come: Assyria, Egypt, Pathros, Ethiopia, Elam, Shinar, Hamath, and the coastlands of the sea (Isa 11:11). Two details make this list particularly appealing as a source or model for the list in Acts 2. First, Isaiah's geographic tour occurs as part of a larger passage that by Luke's day had come to be recognized as a messianic prophecy. Here Isaiah speaks of a "shoot [that] shall come out from the stump of Jesse, and a branch [that] shall grow out of his roots" (Isa 11:1). Endowed with God's spirit, the divine agent will judge with righteousness. Second, the list makes explicit mention of Elam and Egypt, both of which appear in the list of nations in Acts 2.

Scholars have also proposed Jewish writers of the Second Temple period as possible models if not the exact source for the list in Acts. These sources employ their lists for various purposes. A list in Sibylline Oracle 3.158–61 describes the ten successive kingdoms, beginning with kingdom of Cronos, that have held world domination: "But then as time pursued its cyclic course the kingdom of Egypt arose, then that of the Persians, Medes, and Ethiopians, and Assyrian, Babylon, then that of the Macedonians, of Egypt again, then of Rome" (cf. Sibylline Oracles 3.167–73; 5.111–35).

Philo of Alexandria supplies a list of nations inhabited by Jews. In his treatise the *Embassy to Gaius*, he writes:

> While Jerusalem is my native city she is also the mother city not of one country Judea, but of most of the others in virtue of the colonies sent out at diverse times to the neighboring lands: Egypt, Phoenicia, Syria, Pamphylia, Cilicia, most of Asia up to Bithynia and the corners of Pontus, also Europe, Thessaly, Boeotia, Macedonia, Aetolia, Attica, Argos, Corinth, and most of the best parts of the Peloponnese. (Philo, *Embassy to Gaius* 281–82)

The list concludes with a note that Jews live both on the mainlands and in the islands, including Crete. Philo's description of the many lands inhabited by Jews and the list of nations in Acts 2 bear some striking similarities: the general geographic progression moves from east to west; both share specific sites such as Egypt, Pamphylia, Asia, Pontus, and Crete; and both conclude with a mention of the mainland (Arabia in the case of Acts 2) and the islands (Philo, *Embassy to Gaius* 283). Finally, although neither author provides a complete catalog of the nations known to have existed in the first century, both adduce their respective lists to support certain universal claims. For Philo, the list illustrates that Jews inhabit every part of the world. Acts, as Tertullian understood and as I will discuss in greater detail below, uses its list to denote that Jesus holds dominion in every part of the world.

In 1948 Stefan Weinstock proposed another possible source for the list of nations.[16] Building on earlier work published by Franz Cumont and unpublished notes by F. C. Burkitt, Weinstock argued that the locations mentioned in Acts derive from astrological geography in which each sign of the zodiac was thought to influence or control a certain geographic region. One of the simplest and arguably earliest examples of this tradition comes from the astrologer Paul of Alexandria, whose list reads as follows:

Ares	Persia
Taurus	Babylonia
Gemini	Cappadocia
Cancer	Armenia
Leo	Asia
Virgo	Greece and Ionia
Libra	Libya and Cyrene
Scorpio	Italy
Sagittarius	Cilicia and Crete
Capricorn	Syria
Aquarius	Egypt
Pisces	Red Sea and India

Obviously what attracted Weinstock's eye were the numerous sites — Persia/Parthia, Cappadocia, Asia, Egypt, Libya, Cyrene, Crete — shared by this list and the list in Acts. According to Weinstock, both lists were meant to convey an idea of "the whole world."[17] Although Paul of Alexandria wrote in the fourth century c.e., long after Acts, the list

---

16. S. Weinstock, "The Geographical Catalogue in Acts 2:9–11," *Journal of Roman Studies* 38 (1948): 43–46.

17. Ibid., 45. See also G. Lüdemann, *Early Christianity according to the Traditions in Acts* (Minneapolis: Fortress, 1987), 40–41.

betrays elements of a much earlier period.[18] Weinstock argued that Acts and Paul of Alexandria most likely drew from a common astrological tradition. Many years later, Bruce Metzger subjected Weinstock's argument to a careful critique. He concluded that Paul's list cannot be proven to antedate Acts and that the "two lists [are] no closer than would be expected if two ancient authors independently drew up lists comprising a dozen or fifteen representative countries and peoples."[19] Metzger does not offer an alternative suggestion for the source of the list of nations in Acts 2, although he finds the possibility of a "list kept by leaders of the church in Antioch of lands to which Christian missions had been sent prior to about the year 50" c.e. to be an "interesting speculation."[20]

One final possible *Vorlage* deserves our attention. Scholars have not missed the apparent similarities between the list of nations in Acts 2 and the genealogy of Noah's descendants in Gen 10. The passage lists not only Noah's sons, but his grandsons and great-grandsons along with references to the lands they inhabit. Each major section concludes with the note that these are the descendants of one of the sons of Noah by their families, their languages, their lands, and their nations (10:2–31).[21] The biblical list receives considerable attention and elaboration in the Book of Jubilees (8:10–9:13). It should come as no surprise that Goulder once made a strong case in favor of this biblical passage as the source for the list of nations in Acts 2. In his book *Type and History in Acts,* he wrote that the "Pentecost peoples are coterminous with Genesis 10 peoples" (154). The thirteen nations listed in Acts (minus Crete and Arabia, which Goulder argued are later emendations) represent the twelve Gentile nations and the Jews and offer a foretaste of the "twelve gentile 'tribes' to be included in the New Israel at the final harvesting"

---

18. In addition to Weinstock, others (e.g., Cumont and classicist and poet A. E. Houseman) believe this list to be of significant antiquity. See the summaries in B. M. Metzger, "Ancient Astrological Geography and Acts 2:9–11," in *Apostolic History and the Gospel* (ed. W. W. Gasque and R. P. Martin; Grand Rapids: Eerdmans, 1970), 127–30.

19. Ibid., 131.

20. Here Metzger refers to the analysis of B. Reicke. See ibid., 132.

21. On this list of people and similar biblical lists, see E. C. Hostetter, *Nations Mightier and More Numerous* (Richland Hills, Tex.: Bibal, 1995). For a more recent attempt to connect Genesis 10 and Acts 2, see James M. Scott, "Acts 2.9–11 as an Anticipation of the Mission to the Gentiles," in *The Mission of the Early Church to Jews and Gentiles* (ed. J. Ådna and H. Kvalbein; Tübingen: Mohr Siebeck, 2000), 87–123.

(*THA* 155). Goulder and others support the connection between Gen 10 and Acts 2 by noting that the Genesis account juxtaposes a list of nations with the story of the tower of Babel (*THA* 158). Whereas Gen 11 speaks of the confusion of languages, the linguistic miracle of Pentecost marks the "reversal of the curse of Babel."[22] As Goulder notes, "What God had divided and broken at Babel, he restored at Pentecost; unity, comprehensibility, one tongue are returned through the coming of the Spirit" (*THA* 158). The correspondence between Gen 10 and Acts 2 is intriguing, but faces significant problems. The geographic names bare little resemblance from one text to the next. Moreover, the giving of the Spirit at Pentecost does not return humanity to the single universal language that existed before Babel. The newfound ability of the disciples to speak in a multitude of tongues suggests that the word of God is spoken and can be understood in any language. The value of Gen 10–11 for our understanding of Acts 2, therefore, remains questionable.

Despite many careful and imaginative efforts by scholars over the years, we remain no closer to the elusive goal of identifying the origin of the list of nations in Acts 2. The source from which Acts drew the fifteen names has not been identified and may never be known. Even if we could settle on the one, precise source, we would not necessarily be any closer to reconstructing the meaning of the list of nations for Acts. Rather than asking source-critical questions (where did the list come from?), we should be inquiring into the list's function. What purpose does the list of nations have in the narrative context of Acts 2 and in the larger ideological framework of Luke-Acts? The previous discussion has suggested several possibilities: the list in Acts denotes the fulfillment of biblical prophecy, the stellar powers representing universal dominion, and the return to an earlier and more universal state of human existence. None, however, seems particularly apt in explaining Tertullian's use of the list as evidence for Jesus' world dominion. Nor, I suggest, do these options hold much value for understanding Acts itself. To gain a better perspective on the function of the list of nations in Acts, I wish to consider the lists of nations that served as a vehicle for certain forms of

---

22. Bruce, *Acts of the Apostles*, 86.

political propaganda, particularly as used by and applied to the Roman Empire.

In addition to the biblical texts, Second Temple Jewish writings, and astrological tables mentioned above, various forms of Roman propaganda commonly employed lists of nations. Literary texts, monuments, and processions frequently wrote out, inscribed, or displayed images of those nations that had been incorporated, either willingly or (as was more often the case) by force into the Roman Empire. These lists drew their inspiration from and owed their existence to the wealth of geographic information gathered by Herodotus, Eratosthanes, Artemidorus, Strabo, Pomponius Mela, Pliny the Elder, Ptolemy, and many others. These writers combined calculations of distances and physical dimensions with descriptions of topographical features and ethnographic studies of the people who lived there to produce descriptive accounts of various regions, manuals for travelers, and maps. Military campaigns and political acquisitions, such as the conquests of Alexander the Great in the fourth century B.C.E. and the expansion of the Roman provincial system in the second and first centuries B.C.E., contributed to both the interest in and the need for accurate geographic information.[23] It became particularly important for the Roman government to have a reliable account of its territorial holdings in order to govern efficiently, exploit its resources, and gather and transmit information to the far-flung reaches of its empire.

Geography served more than scientific and administrative purposes. Geographers and the information they presented often advanced political agendas. Strabo, born in the middle of the first century B.C.E., recognized that geography had importance not only for explorers, generals, and hunters, but also on the "life and needs of rulers" (1.1.16–18). The ancient state most adept in employing geographic information for political purposes was Rome.[24] By the second century B.C.E., if not a century earlier, Rome had firmly established an agenda of imperial ex-

---

23. On ancient geography, see J. O. Thomson, *History of Ancient Geography* (Cambridge: Cambridge University Press, 1948); O. A. W. Dilke, *Greek and Roman Maps* (Ithaca: Cornell University Press, 1985); R. Syme, "Military Geography at Rome," *Classical Antiquity* 7 (1988): 227–51; K. Clarke, *Between Geography and History: Hellenistic Constructions of the Roman World* (Oxford: Oxford University Press, 2000).

24. C. Nicolet, *Space, Geography, and Politics in the Early Roman Empire* (trans. H. Leclerc; Ann Arbor: University of Michigan Press, 1991), 29–56.

pansion.[25] Second-century historian Polybius marveled that in a short span of time Rome succeeded in "subjecting nearly the whole inhabited world (*oikoumenē*) to their sole government — a thing unique in history" (1.1.5; see also 6.50.6; 15.9.5).[26] By the end of the second century B.C.E., the title *masters of the world* (*kyrioi tēs oikoumenēs*) had been firmly applied to Rome (Plutarch, *Tiberius Gracchus* 9.6). Following the conquests of Pompey in the east, the idea of Rome as ruler of the inhabited world became commonplace.[27] Cicero several times praises Pompey and Caesar for extending Rome's boundaries and often speaks "as if Rome already ruled all peoples or the whole *orbis terrarum*."[28] Pompey, Caesar, and most magnificently Augustus heralded Rome's supreme position in the world. Rome's friends and supporters spouted similar thoughts and expressions. Josephus, for instance, relates the dramatic speech of Agrippa II in which the king attempted to persuade Jews not to revolt against Rome (*Jewish War* 2.345–401).[29] Agrippa begins by noting that the primary reasons for rebellion — hatred of the procurators and desire for liberty — either do not justify war against Rome or are no longer practical. He then parades before their ears the numerous peoples who, once mighty, have become servants of Rome and asks how they, the Jews, can withstand such a superior force. The voice of realism, Agrippa reminds his audience that "almost every nation under the sun does homage to the Roman arms" (*Jewish War* 2.380).

Affirmations and displays of Rome's supremacy intensified during the time of Augustus. Official, or at least semiofficial, Augustan literature claimed universal domination as Rome's inherent destiny. Virgil's *Aeneid* represents a *locus classicus* for this perspective. In the first book of this

---

25. For a maximalist analysis of Rome's imperialist intentions, see W. V. Harris, *War and Imperialism in Republican Rome, 327–70 BC* (Oxford: Oxford University Press, 1979).

26. On Polybius's understanding of Roman policy, see Harris, *War and Imperialism*, 107–17; Clarke, *Between Geography and History*, 77–128.

27. See the references in Nicolet, *Space, Geography, and Politics*, 31.

28. P. A. Brunt, "Laus Imperii," in *Imperialism in the Ancient World* (ed. P. D. A. Garnsey and C. R. Whittaker; Cambridge: Cambridge University Press, 1978), 168, with specific references to Cicero's writings on 162–68.

29. See the discussion in S. Schwartz, *Josephus and Judean Politics* (Columbia Studies in the Classical Tradition 18; Leiden: Brill, 1990), 133–36; and T. Rajak, "Friends, Romans, Subjects: Agrippa II's Speech in Josephus's *Jewish War*," in *Images of Empire* (ed. L. Alexander; Journal for the Study of the Old Testament Supplement 122; Sheffield: Sheffield Academic Press, 1991), 122–34.

nationalist epic, Jupiter utters his famous prophecy that Rome will pos-
sess an empire without end (*Aeneid* 1.279). Later in the poem, Aeneas
travels to the underworld where his guide, his recently deceased father
Anchises, describes the numerous territories acquired by Augustus. So
vast is the space that Hercules himself had never crossed it (*Aeneid*
6.791–803). Virgil was not alone in his estimation of Roman power.
Livy claimed that Rome's destiny was to be head of the world (1.16.7).
Strabo's efforts to write his "account of the whole world known to the
Romans" both reflected and contributed toward the voice of Roman
imperialism.[30] First-century B.C.E. historian and biographer Cornelius
Nepos celebrated Rome's desire to rule the world (*Atticus* 3.3; 20.5). Official decrees and coins with images of the goddess Roma astride a globe,
a symbol of universal domination, also advanced the idea that Rome
was master of the inhabited world.[31] Public maps provided a graphic
display to support this defining ideology of the Roman Empire. Perhaps
the most famous example of the genre was the map erected on the wall
of the Porticus Vipsania, begun by Marcus Agrippa and completed after
his death.[32] It included the names of twenty-four regions and illustrated
that "the empire had (theoretically) been expanded to the limits of the
orbis terrarum."[33]

Among the various ways to promote the claim that Rome ruled the
entire world, the listing of foreign nations or peoples falling under Rome's
sway proved to be one of the more frequent and effective. In the middle
of the first century, Pompey made frequent use of such lists to extol his
own accomplishments and Rome's new territorial dimensions. According
to Pliny the Elder, he announced the procession celebrating his triumphs
in the east in the following manner:

> After having rescued the sea coast from pirates and restored to
> the Roman people the command of the sea, (Pompey) celebrated
> a triumph over Asia, Pontus, Armenia, Paphlagonia, Cappadocia,

---

30. Clarke, *Between Geography and History,* 344.
31. Nicolet, *Space, Geography, and Politics,* 34–38.
32. The map, no longer extant, is described by Pliny the Elder. For a list of passages and discussion,
see Dilke, *Greek and Roman Maps,* 41–53.
33. Nicolet, *Space, Geography, and Politics,* 111.

Cilicia, Syria, the Scythians, Jews, and Albanians, Iberia, the is-
land of Crete, the Basternae, and in addition to these, over King
Mithradates and Tigranes. (Pliny, *Naturalis historia* 7.98)

He memorialized his achievement in an inscription dedicated perhaps in
the temple of Venus:

> Pompey... having liberated the seacoast of the inhabited world...
> [and] delivered from siege the kingdom of Ariobarzanes, Galatia
> and the lands and provinces lying beyond it, Asia, and Bithynia;
> who gave protection to Paphlagonia and Pontus, Armenia and
> Achaia, as well as Iberia, Colchis, Mesopotamia, Sophene, and
> Gordyene; brought into subjection Darius king of the Medes, Ar-
> toles king of the Iberians, Aristobulus king of the Jews, Aretas king
> of the Nabatean Arabs, Syria bordering on Cilicia, Judea, Arabia,
> the province of Cyrene, the Acheans, the Iozygi, the Soani, the
> Heniochi, and the other tribes along the seacoast between Colchis
> and the Maeotic Sea. (Diodorus Siculus 40.4)

Through this list, Pompey presented his actions as having "extended the
frontiers of the empire to the limits of the earth" (Diodorus Siculus 40.4).
Lists of nations came in many forms. In addition to the verbal lists in
literary texts and inscriptions, nations were cataloged using statues and
other artistic displays. Around the same time as his triumphal procession, Pompey commissioned a set of fourteen statues of the *nationes* that
he brought under Roman rule. This representational listing of nations
decorated his theater in Rome (Pliny, *Naturalis historia* 36.41; Suetonius,
Nero 46).

In the new political reality of the principate, literary and visual cata-
logs of Roman possessions became more prominent. Writers of the early
principate, such as Virgil (*Aeneid* 6.780ff.), Curtius Rufus (6.3.3), and
Pliny the Elder (*Naturalis historia* 5.132–33), evoked the glory of the
empire with their own lists of nations.[34] In addition to the literary cat-
alogs, epigraphic and representational displays bolstered the declaration

---

34. Lists continued to have an important role in political propaganda in the later principate. See
the nations recorded as Augustan victories in Dio 51–56.

of Roman power.[35] The map of Agrippa, mentioned above, "may have been in the form of a list of places, rather than a graphic representation of the world."[36] We find such visual inventories in relief fragments of small ethnic figures decorating the Ara Pacis, the Augustan monument dedicated in 9 B.C.E. to commemorate the peace, stability, and prosperity brought about by the *Pax Augusta;*[37] in the *Portico ad Nationes* with its images (*simulacra*) of all the *gentes* within the empire (Servius, *Ad Aeneid* 8.721; Pliny, *Naturalis historia* 36.39); and in the forum of Augustus where inscriptions (*tituli*) listed the various regions comprising the Roman Empire (Suetonius, *Augustus* 31.8; Velleius 2.39.2). At Augustus's funeral, images of all the *ethnē* acquired by Augustus were carried in procession (Tacitus, *Annals* 1.8.4; Dio 56.34.2–3). Lists of nations, whether in literary texts, inscriptions, or statuary collections, impressed upon their audience the overwhelming power and universal authority of the Roman Empire. By the first century C.E., these lists, similar to the one found in Acts 2, provided a common and forceful means to proclaim Rome's position as ruler of the world.

The most famous list of nations and example of Augustan political geography emerges in the *Res Gestae*. Augustus instructed that this record of his achievements be inscribed near his mausoleum after his death. The text begins with the words *rerum gestarum divi Augusti, quibus orbem terrarum imperio populi Romani subiiecit:* "The accomplishments of the deified Augustus by which he subjected the inhabited world under the empire of the Roman people." Much of what appears in this document records "the direct or indirect completion of the conquest of the world."[38] In chapters 25–33, Augustus tallies fifty-five geographical places conquered, pacified, added, or otherwise dominated by Rome. Not only does the *Res Gestae* offer us an important example of how Roman leaders transmitted their ideas of political geography, it also demonstrates how this image was accepted and propagated beyond the walls of the

---

35. See the discussion in R. R. R. Smith, "*Simulacra Gentium:* The *Ethne* From the Sebasteion at Aphrodisias," *Journal of Roman Studies* 78 (1988): 71–77.

36. Clarke, *Between Geography and History*, 8–9.

37. D. Castriota, *The Ara Pacis Augustae* (Princeton: Princeton University Press, 1995), 6.

38. Nicolet, *Space, Geography, and Politics*, 29.

city itself.[39] The surviving texts of the *Res Gestae* have come down to us in Latin and Greek records erected in three cities of Asia Minor: Ancyra, Pisidian Antioch, and Apollonia. The presence of copies of the *Res Gestae* in central Asia Minor illustrates how Rome's image as ruler of the world spread quickly to the places and the people who comprised its empire. The practice of amassing geographical data as a way to champion the vision of universal rule was not restricted to official Roman circles. Rome's friends and allies recognized the value such lists had in creating strong bonds between themselves and the princeps.[40] In Jerusalem, Herod, friend and client-king of Rome, built a theater displaying the inscriptions and trophies of the peoples whom Augustus had conquered (Josephus, *Antiquities* 15.272).[41]

For another example, we turn to the *sebasteion* in the Carian city of Aphrodisias. Aphrodisias has become well known to scholars of the New Testament and ancient Judaism in large part from the now famous God-fearer inscription.[42] A stone pillar inscribed on two sides contains a list of persons somehow associated with a Jewish organization which identifies itself as a *dekany*. On side b, we read the names along with patronymics, official positions, and sometimes the occupations of fifty-two men who are designated as *theosebeis*, a Greek term often translated "God-fearer." God-fearers, as the accepted view would have it, "were those people who hovered on the fringe of the synagogue, sufficiently interested to remain there, yet unwilling to jump the final hurdle, male circumcision."[43] God-fearers, of course, play an important role in Acts of the Apostles. Cornelius, the centurion converted by Peter in Acts 10, is described as a man who feared God (*phoboumenos ton theon*). Scholars have often understood this expression as a synonym for the term *theose-*

---

39. The text itself appears to have been intended primarily for the people of Rome. See P. A. Brunt and J. M. Moore (eds.), *Res Gestae Divi Augusti* (Oxford: Oxford University Press, 1967), 4.

40. D. Braund, *Rome and the Friendly King* (London: St. Martin's, 1984); P. Zanker, *The Power of Images in the Age of Augustus* (Ann Arbor: University of Michigan Press, 1988), 297–333.

41. On Herod's relations with Rome, particularly Augustus, see P. Richardson, *Herod: King of the Jews and Friend of the Romans* (Columbia: University of South Carolina Press, 1996), 226–34.

42. J. Reynolds and R. Tannenbaum, *Jews and Godfearers at Aphrodisias* (Cambridge Philological Society Supplement 12; Cambridge: Cambridge University Press, 1987).

43. J. Lieu, "Do God-fearers Make Good Christians?" in *Crossing the Boundaries: Essays in Biblical Interpretation in Honour of Michael D. Goulder* (ed. S. E. Porter, P. Joyce, and D. E. Orton; Biblical Interpretation Series 8; Leiden: Brill, 1994), 329.

beis and thus have identified the first Gentile to convert to Christianity as a God-fearer. God-fearers appear with great regularity in Acts. The synagogues in which Paul preached were most often filled with crowds of both Jews and God-fearers. The Aphrodisias inscription, then, has added to our understanding of the religious and social interactions between Jews and polytheists in the ancient world.

Archeologists digging in Aphrodisias, however, have unearthed much more than this one inscription. In addition to the magnificent theater, bathhouse, and stadium, Aphrodisias possessed a *sebasteion,* or imperial temple. The term *sebasteion* refers to a variety of structures in the ancient world — temples, shrines, or sanctuaries — where persons conducted rituals devoted to the deified Roman emperors. *Sebasteia* were found in many cities of Asia Minor, including Pergamum, Smyrna, Ephesus, Miletus, and Sardis. An inscription from Aphrodisias referring to *ho sebasteios naos* (the imperial temple) has been known since the nineteenth century (*Corpus inscriptionum graecarum* 2839 1.2). Until 1979, however, no known building could claim the honor. In that year, an archeological team led by Kenin Erim uncovered an elaborate structure that it identified as the *sebasteion.*[44] The identification receives strong endorsement from references in the dedicatory inscriptions to the *theoi sebastoi* (divine Augusti) and statuary and reliefs depicting members of the imperial family, often in the guise or shown with the attributes of divine beings.

The building clearly served to glorify Rome and the imperial family. It rested in the heart of the urban landscape of Aphrodisias, in proximity to other major structures, including the temple of Aphrodite (the city's patron deity), the agora, and an impressive theater. Building of the *sebasteion* began during the reign of Tiberius and probably concluded before the end of the reign of Nero. Funding for its construction came from two wealthy families whose involvement with the imperial cult also

---

44. Published information on the *sebasteion* includes J. Reynolds, "The Origins and Beginning of Imperial Cult at Aphrodisias," *Proceedings of the Cambridge Philological Society* 206 (1980): 70–82; idem, "New Evidence for the Imperial Cult in Julio-Claudian Aphrodisias," *Zeitschrift für Papyrologie und Epigraphik* 43 (1981): 317–27; idem, "Further Information on the Imperial Cult at Aphrodisias," *Studii Classice* 24 (1986): 109–17; R. R. R. Smith, "The Imperial Reliefs from the Sebasteion at Aphrodisias," *Journal of Roman Studies* 77 (1987): 88–138; idem, "*Simulacra Gentium.*"

included appointments as high priest or priestess for at least three of its members.

The existence of a sacred complex where the worship of the Roman emperors took place reflects well the political and religious consciousness of Aphrodisias. For most of the Roman republic, Aphrodisias existed in relative obscurity. It first appears in the extant historical record during the time of Sulla, early in the first century B.C.E. Contemporary epigraphic and numismatic materials record the city's official designation as the "sympolity of Plarasa," an otherwise unknown site, and, in subordinate position, "Aphrodisias."[45] By the beginning of the principate, however, Aphrodisias had emerged as an important city in the region of Caria and in the eyes of Rome. Its fortunes rose with the centralization of Roman power and authority beginning with Julius Caesar. The Julian family had long considered Venus/Aphrodite as its divine progenitor, a view expressed most famously in the *Aeneid*. In several inscriptions, including one from the city itself, Aphrodite is referred to as *promētōr* (first-mother) of the *sebastoi*.[46] The prominence given to Venus/Aphrodite by both city and princeps had practical effects for both parties. Roman leaders from Caesar on took special interest in a city whose eponymous deity bolstered the divine character of the imperial family. Augustus once described Aphrodisias as "the one city of Asia which I have taken for my own."[47] In turn, Aphrodisias proudly boasted of its exceptional relationship with Rome. A wall inscribed with numerous official documents includes several letters from Augustus. In one to the magistrates, council, and people of Ephesus and in another to the people of Samos, he, *inter alia*, denies those cities privileges that he had earlier bestowed upon Aphrodisias.[48] Additionally, the city provided Rome, especially the Julio-Claudian rulers, with unwavering military support. Aphrodisias sided with Rome against foreign enemies like Mithradates and allied itself with the Caesarian party. In return,

---

45. The combination constituted a new polis with one board of magistrates, one council, and one demos. The year 88 marks the *terminus ante quem* for the sympolity. Caria became a part of the province of Asia probably in 129 or soon thereafter. See J. Reynolds, *Aphrodisias and Rome* (London: Society for the Promotion of Roman Studies, 1982), docs. 1–4, 6, 8.

46. Ibid., 182.

47. Ibid., doc. 9.

48. Ibid., docs. 12–13.

Rome granted Aphrodisias several privileges, including immunity from imperial taxation, the right of asylum, and exemption from provincial liturgies. The *sebasteion*, therefore, should be seen as one facet in a complex religious and political interchange between imperial Rome and the city of Aphrodisias.

The *sebasteion* consists of four interrelated structures oriented on an east-west axis: at the far west stood a propylon or gateway; at the far east stood the actual temple or shrine.[49] Enclosing the space between them were two porticoes, one on the north and one on the south, separated from each other by a paved area fourteen meters wide. Each side was approximately eighty meters long and consisted of three superimposed stories reaching a total height of about twelve meters. The intercolumniations of the first level were composed of undecorated marble slabs separated by engaged Doric columns. The second and third stories consisted of panels with elaborate reliefs depicting deities, scenes from classical mythology, and members of the imperial family. The panels, estimated to have totaled 190, can be divided into several groups: on the south were mythological scenes, including depictions of Leda and the swan, Dionysus as an infant being presented to his nurse Myssa, Io and Argos, Apollo at the oracle at Delphi, and Bellerophon with Pegasus. One of the panels closest to the temple offers, no doubt intentionally, a visual narration of a story that bespeaks the mythological foundation of Rome: Aeneas's flight from Troy. Along the north portico, the top register featured, at least in part, universal allegories of which only two survive: personifications of Hemera (Day) and Okeanos (Ocean).

Many of the surviving reliefs and their attendant inscriptions celebrate Rome's military victories and its position as ruler of the world. The south portico exhibits portraits of Augustus and other members of the Julio-Claudian family. Many of these reliefs depict an image of the princeps as a victorious military leader or receptor of the symbols of world dominion. Augustus, for instance, strides forward receiving from divine figures objects symbolizing the earth's bounty and expanse: a cornucopia from earth and a ship's steering oar from the sea. In another

---

49. For a more complete description of the *sebasteion*, its architecture, and artwork, see Smith, "Imperial Reliefs"; and idem, *"Simulacra Gentium."*

panel, Augustus and Nike flank a trophy of armor with bound captives beneath. Similar juxtapositions of imperial figures and personifications of a vanquished people appear often in these panels. Two additional reliefs recount historical victories of the Roman military. Claudius stands over the defeated figure of Britannia, while Nero dominates a collapsed Armenia who rests between the wide-striding legs of the princeps.

Rome often articulated an ideology of universal domination by listing those nations subject to it. The *sebasteion* also employed this form of propaganda with a large group of ethnic personifications and inscriptions. Each panel is composed of two elements. At the bottom was a base decorated with a garlanded mask accompanied by an inscription identifying a particular people (*ethnos*). Standing on the base is a female figure, each one well differentiated by its drapery, pose, and sometimes distinctive attributes, such as facial features and hair style. Sixteen of the approximately fifty original inscriptions survive and include *ethnē* ranging geographically from Spain in the west to the Alpine regions, Dacia, the Balkans, Egypt, Arabia, and the major islands of the Mediterranean — Crete, Cyprus, and Sicily. Judea was also included in this verbal and visual list of nations.[50] The various peoples and places have been explained as part of a series illustrating the victories of Augustus. The concept of victory, however, should be understood as more than armed conflict. Many of the peoples are known to have been defeated militarily by Augustus. Others were not so much conquered as they were incorporated through diplomatic or other nonviolent methods. The latter category included Sicily and possibly Crete, Cyprus, and Judea, which became a Roman province following the deposition of Archelaus in 6 C.E. A few of the *ethnē* existed completely beyond the boundaries of the Roman Empire in the first century. Arabia, for instance, was not incorporated into the empire until the second century, that is, after the completion of the *sebasteion*. Its inclusion in this context reminds us that the *sebasteion*'s list of nations existed more to meet the needs of Roman rhetoric than to describe the historical reality of the first century. Aphrodisias's walk of nations and the related examples surveyed above demonstrate that a

---

50. Smith, *"Simulacra Gentium,"* 55–57.

list of nations, whether in literary, epigraphic, or representational form, were an often used and well-known method to represent the boundless geographic expanses under Roman rule and to declare Rome's position as ruler of the world.

In the first century, geographic writings and, more specifically, lists of nations were a means to persuade as well as inform. These lists, as much as any legion or provincial unit, constructed the territorial dimensions of the Roman Empire. Tertullian, the son of a Roman military officer and well read and educated in law, literature, and philosophy, certainly knew of Rome's claim to be ruler of the world and most likely was aware of how literature, monuments, and processions employed lists of nations to promote this ideology.[51] It is not surprising, therefore, that he read the list in Acts 2 within the context of Roman political propaganda. For Tertullian, of course, the list of nations in Acts presented the proof for the universal rule not of Caesar, but of Christ. Let me suggest that Tertullian's geopolitical interpretation was far from unique and provides an appropriate lens for viewing Luke-Acts.

Three well-known features of Luke-Acts suggest an awareness of geopolitical propaganda. Luke-Acts presents Jesus as a universal figure. The angels who appear before the shepherds in the birth narrative announce that they "bring good news of great joy *for all the people*" (Luke 2:10). The righteous and devout Simeon recognizes that Jesus is the "salvation which [God has] prepared in the presence *of all peoples,* a light for revelation to the Gentiles" (2:30–31). The Lucan genealogy traces Jesus' lineage back to Adam, the paternal progenitor of all humanity (3:38). John the Baptist announces that "*all flesh* shall see the salvation of God" (3:6). In the last passage, the author of Luke drew upon the Gospel of Mark as a source for his story of John the Baptist. Mark, too, includes a quotation from Isaiah. Whereas Mark ends with "and the crooked shall be made straight," Luke continues the quotation and includes the reference to all flesh. Finally, Acts opens with Jesus commissioning the apostles to be his witnesses in Jerusalem, Judea, and Samaria and to the

51. On the ideology of world dominion in the second century C.E., see V. Nutton, "The Beneficial Ideology," in *Imperialism in the Ancient World* (ed. P. D. A. Garnsey and C. R. Whittaker; Cambridge: Cambridge University Press, 1978), 209–21.

end of the earth (Acts 1:8). The list of nations, which soon follows, reinforces the universal character of Jesus' rule.

Not only do Jesus' life and death have universal significance, the story of Jesus and the expansion of the church take place as major events in world history. Jesus' birth occurs during a worldwide (*pasan tēn oikoumenēn*) census decreed by Emperor Augustus (Luke 2:1). John the Baptist begins his preaching around the Jordan River in the fifteenth year of Emperor Tiberius (3:1). The prophecy of Agabus regarding a universal famine took place during the reign of Claudius (Acts 11:27–28). In Corinth, Paul meets Priscilla and Aquila who had recently left Rome "because Claudius had ordered all Jews to leave" (18:2). In his appearance before Agrippa II and Roman procurator Festus, Paul delivers a stirring speech that sums up the sentiment suggested by these passages. The importance of Jesus and the church is not restricted to a single people or region of the empire, for "this was not done in a corner" (26:26). Rather, Luke-Acts narrates events that concern the entire world.

Finally, Luke-Acts identifies Jesus by titles that bore unmistakable associations with the Roman princeps. According to Luke-Acts, Jesus is Savior (Luke 2:11; Acts 5:31; 13:23) and bringer of peace (Luke 1:79; 2:14; Acts 10:36). The same titles and benefits were claimed by and for Augustus. An inscription from Priene recording a decree of the Asian league speaks of Augustus as savior, one "who has made war to cease and who shall put everything in peaceful order."[52] Together these themes, universal rule, inclusion in world history, and titles of imperial rule demonstrate a pronounced interest in portraying Jesus as the universal Lord and Savior. In the first century, Rome made a similar claim for the princeps and expressed its ideology of universal dominion with a list of nations. Luke-Acts has done likewise. By incorporating a list of nations, a well-established method of geographical propaganda, the author of Luke-Acts presents the story of Pentecost less as the ingathering of Israel and more as a moment to adumbrate the future and inevitable expansion of Christianity and the power of Jesus throughout the world.

---

52. *Inschriften von Priene* 105 (= Supplementum epigraphicum graecum 4.490). See the translation and discussion in F. W. Danker, *Benefactor* (St. Louis: Clayton, 1982), 215–22.

Luke-Acts not only models the list of nations and other attributes of Jesus from imperial propaganda, but uses these elements as a way to respond to Rome's claim of universal dominion. Whereas Rome claimed Caesar to be the true lord and savior, the bringer of peace, the one who holds dominion over the entire world, Luke-Acts identifies Jesus in these roles. Not only do Luke-Acts and Rome contend over who is the true ruler of the world, they both attribute divine will — the God of Israel for Luke-Acts and Jupiter, Venus, and other members of the Roman pantheon for Rome — as the guarantor of their respective ruler's position.[53] In this way, political geography combines with sacred geography, and political power and cosmic power thereby become identified as one.[54] The contention between Rome and Luke-Acts over claims of universal rule becomes an example of mimetic desire.[55] René Girard explains:

> In the varieties of desire examined by us, we have encountered not only a subject and an object but a third presence as well: the rival.... The rival desires the same object as the subject, and to assert the primacy of the rival can lead to only one conclusion. Rivalry does not arise because of the fortuitous convergence of two desires on a single object; rather *the subject desires the object because the rival desires it.* In desiring an object the rival alerts the subject to the desirability of the object. The rival, then, serves as a model for the subject, not only in regard to such secondary matters as style and opinions but also, and more essentially, in regard to desires.[56]

In our study, Luke-Acts (subject) desires to present Jesus as ruler of the world (object), in contrast to the Roman Empire (rival). Luke-Acts expresses this desire in part by using the same method developed by

---

53. For a discussion of divine will and Roman imperialism, see Brunt, "Laus Imperii," 165–68.

54. D. R. Edwards, *Religion and Power: Pagans, Jews, and Christians in the Greek East* (Oxford: Oxford University Press, 1996), 72–90.

55. The analysis of V. Robbins has been very helpful here; see his "Luke-Acts: A Mixed Population Seeks a Home in the Roman Empire," in *Images of Empire* (ed. L. Alexander; Journal for the Study of the Old Testament Supplement 122; Sheffield: Sheffield Academic Press, 1991), 203–5. While agreeing with his use of Girard's theory, I come to a different conclusion about Luke-Acts. Rather than building alliances, Luke-Acts offers its audience an alterative reality in which Christ and not Caesar is ruler of the world.

56. R. Girard, *Violence and the Sacred* (trans. P. Gregory; Baltimore: Johns Hopkins University Press, 1977), 145 (emphasis original).

its rival, a list of nations. Through the list of nations in Acts 2, Luke-Acts imitates the well-known political rhetoric in its desire to reject and counter the ideology that Rome and its princeps acted as ruler of the world. This honor went not to Rome, but to the true Lord and Savior, Jesus Christ. I am not suggesting that the inclusion of the Gentiles begins in Acts 2. As most scholars recognize, this major event commences with the conversion of Cornelius in Acts 10. At several points, such as the prophecy of Simeon that salvation has come to all people, Jesus' commission to the apostles to be his witnesses to the end of the earth, or the story of the Gentile Ethiopian eunuch in Acts 8, Luke-Acts foreshadows this event, using the narrative present to disclose the future of Jesus' universal domination.[57] The list of nations functions similarly.

Although many peoples in the first century celebrated Rome's territorial authority and endorsed its methods of geopolitical propaganda, not all shared this view. Dissident voices questioned Rome's supremacy and the legitimacy of the emperor's authority. The first Jewish revolt represents only one of the more violent manifestations of this opposition. More common were the numerous forms of resistance from senatorial and intellectual circles, sometimes resulting in conspiratorial activities against the early emperors.[58] Luke-Acts should be included among those writings that expressed opposition to the Roman Empire. I am not suggesting that the author called for military resistance or anticipated the imminent collapse of the Roman principate. Rather, in using a list of nations and titles such as Lord and Savior, Luke-Acts means to delegitimate and therefore to oppose Rome's claim to universal dominion.

This conclusion runs counter to many studies that examine the purpose of Luke-Acts. Two common views posit Luke-Acts as an *apologia pro*

---

57. Schneider, *Die Apostelgeschichte*, 1.251.

58. A. Giovannini (ed.), *Opposition et résistances à l'empire d'Auguste à Trajan* (Entretiens sur l'antiquité classique 33; Geneva: Hardt, 1987); K. A. Raaflaub and L. J. Samons II, "Opposition to Augustus," in *Between Republic and Empire: Interpretations of Augustus and His Principate* (Berkeley: University of California Press, 1990), 417–54; M. H. Crawford, "Greek Intellectuals and the Roman Aristocracy," in *Images of Empire* (ed. L. Alexander; Journal for the Study of the Old Testament Supplement 122; Sheffield: Sheffield Academic Press, 1991). On Jewish opposition to Rome, see M. Goodman, "Opponents of Rome: Jews and Others," in *Images of Empire* (ed. L. Alexander; Journal for the Study of the Old Testament Supplement 122; Sheffield: Sheffield Academic Press, 1991), 222–38. On early Christian attitudes toward Rome, see K. Wengst, *Pax Romana and the Peace of Jesus Christ* (trans. J. Bowden; London: SCM, 1987).

ecclesia, a defense of Christianity against charges brought by Roman offi-
cials, or an *apologia pro imperio,* a defense of Rome presented to Christians
who are skeptical of the empire's benefits.[59] Although envisioning different audiences, both positions share the understanding that Luke-Acts
is compatible with, if not in support of, the Roman Empire. Although a
detailed analysis must wait for another occasion, let me make the suggestive observation that Luke-Acts fails to present a consistent view of
this and other issues. We encounter a similar difficulty when attempting
to interpret the portrayal of Jews in Luke-Acts. Jews are the ones responsible for the deaths of Jesus and Stephen and for leading the opposition
to Paul. They are also Jesus' dinner hosts and the reasoned voice of the
Pharisee Gamaliel. The differing conclusions presented in recent studies
caution us to acknowledge that the text speaks with a highly nuanced
and multitonal voice.[60] It would be equally difficult and imprecise to
ascribe one purpose to a work of this complexity.

By understanding how and why Rome and its supporters listed the
nations under its dominion, we can hear the list of nations in Acts 2 as it
was perceived certainly early in the third century, as proven by Tertullian,
and very possibly in the first century as well. The ironic use of a well-
known form of geopolitical propaganda creates a very different reality
from that projected by Rome. Luke-Acts presents the reader with a voice
dismissive of the claim that Rome was ruler of the world and speaks
of the true *oikoumenē* created through the Spirit, ruled over by Jesus,
and mapped out by the list of nations in Acts 2. Through a discourse
of resistance, Acts has co-opted Roman propaganda and adapted it to
reinforce the claim that all the nations of the earth now rest under the
dominion, not of Caesar, but of God and his son, Jesus.

---

59. C. H. Talbert, *Luke and the Gnostics* (Nashville: Abingdon, 1966); P. W. Walaskay, *"And So We Came to Rome": The Political Perspective of St. Luke* (Cambridge: Cambridge University Press, 1983); R. Maddox, *The Purpose of Luke-Acts* (Edinburgh: T&T Clark, 1982); and P. F. Esler, *Community and Gospel in Luke-Acts: The Social and Political Motivations of Lucan Theology* (Society for New Testament Studies Monograph 57; Cambridge: Cambridge University Press, 1987).

60. J. Jervell, *Luke and the People of God: A New Look at Luke-Acts* (Minneapolis: Augsburg, 1972); J. T. Sanders, *The Jews in Luke-Acts* (Philadelphia: Fortress, 1987); J. B. Tyson (ed.), *Luke-Acts and the Jewish People* (Minneapolis: Augsburg, 1988); H. Kee, "The Jews in Acts, in *Diaspora Jews and Judaism* (ed. A. J. Overman and R. MacLennan; Atlanta: Scholars Press, 1992), 183–96; G. Gilbert, "The Disappearance of the Gentiles: God-fearers and the Image of the Jews in Luke-Acts," in *Putting Body and Soul Together* (ed. V. Wiles, A. Brown, and G. F. Snyder; Valley Forge, Pa.: Trinity, 1997), 172–84.

SIX

TRANSFORMATION
AND AFTERLIFE

Alan F. Segal

In his provocative book A *Tale of Two Missions*, Michael Goulder finds that ecstasy and visions were an area of controversy between Paul and Peter.[1] While not his most famous piece of scholarship, this book shows Goulder hard at work in his successful teaching career, explaining the difficult context of the New Testament to eager adult students who are continuing their educations after hours. I know that this is a difficult audience, as I have, not always successfully, tried my luck with it myself. So I appreciate Goulder's real accomplishments in making this book so readable and interesting. These are consummate teaching skills. Reading his book is like talking to him. Books like this are frequently underappreciated by other scholars, but I think this book shows an important aspect of his genius. He can express his complicated perceptions in simple, easy to understand, clearly wrought sentences. This is a rare talent among scholars.

In his witty prose, Goulder shows us that he is a master of irony. This book is a very smart piece of work and I have used it for many years with great satisfaction. And I thought that I had understood its position, with which I largely agree, though I have quibbles with some of its details. In other articles Goulder goes yet further, suggesting that there is an ironic and satirical tone in 2 Cor 12. I disagree with that further irony. If Goulder holds that position, it is not evident in A *Tale of Two Missions*. I will take some time later to show why I disagree with

---

1. M. D. Goulder, A *Tale of Two Missions* (London: SCM, 1994).

111

that further interpretation, but in the meantime my difficulty lies in unraveling a literary problem, the subtlety of tracing the source of the irony that Goulder feels in 2 Cor 12:

> The vision thing, as Mr Bush would say, was not new in II Corinthians. Petrines talked about *words of knowledge* in I Cor. 12.8: that is rulings delivered by angels seen in visions, just as *words of wisdom* were rulings delivered by arguments from scripture. Paul says that if the Jewish rulers had *known*, they would not have had Jesus crucified: he was the Lord of Glory, something that *no eye has seen* (I Cor. 2.8f.; Isa. 64.4). *Knowledge*, he says later, is imperfect and temporary: "For now we see through a mirror dimly, but then face to face. Now I *know* in part; then I shall *know* fully, even as I have been fully *known*" (1 Cor. 13.12). But seeing God and the *knowledge* supposed to come from it, do not hold a candle to *love*.[2]

Goulder's acerbic and cutting irony is unmistakable and always well focused. He also gives a prescient description of the Pauline pastoral position. It asks us to consider the nature of the wider context of ecstatic or nonnormal states of consciousness and experience in the church. Obviously, both the Petrine branch and the Pauline branch of the church were open to the prospect of these experiences — more so than many of their Jewish brothers — but, as Goulder tells us, Paul and Peter had different ways of evaluating that experience.

In this essay, I want to show that the basic understanding of Christianity itself comes from ecstatic experience of being in Christ and that it was that revelation which provided the demonstration that Christ had been resurrected and sits next to the father in heaven. It was this experience in Paul that defined the nature of Christ's resurrection and the nature of the Christian afterlife and it was this experience that set the example for Christian community in the Gospels. Each kind of Christian document presents its own interpretation and develops its own language to deal with the religiously altered state of consciousness, but they both depend upon it.

---

2. Ibid., 52–53 (emphasis original).

Transformation into the Christ

Of course, we all know that Paul gives us an example — likely a confessional experience, I think, but Goulder demurs — of religiously altered states of consciousness in 2 Cor 12. But we both agree on one important point: Even if Paul is not giving us his personal mystical experience, he reveals much about the mystical religion as it was experienced in the first century. A great deal of the visionary life of this period dealt with the appearance of what Ezekiel called "the likeness of the image of the glory of the Lord." Paul himself designates Christ as the image of the Lord in 2 Cor 4:4 and Col 1:15 (if it is Pauline), and he mentions the *morphē* (likeness) of God in Phil 2:6.[3] More often he talks of transforming believers into the image of the Son in various ways (Rom 8:29; 2 Cor 3:18; Phil 3:21; 1 Cor 15:49; see also Col 3:9), as we shall see. These passages are critical to understanding Paul's personal experience of conversion, justification, and salvation. They must be seen in closer detail to understand the relationship to Jewish apocalypticism and mysticism, from which they derive their most complete significance for Paul.

Paul's longest discussion of these themes occurs in an unlikely place in 2 Cor 3:18–4:6. Here he assumes the context rather than explaining it completely:

> And we all, with unveiled face, beholding the glory of the Lord, are being changed into his likeness from one degree of glory to another; for this comes from the Lord who is the Spirit (*hēmeis de pantes anakekalymenō prosōpō tēn doxan kyriou katoptrizomenoi tēn autēn eikona metamorphoumetha apo doxēs eis doxan kathaper apo kyriou pneumatos*). Therefore, having this ministry (*tēn diakonian tautēn*) by the mercy of God, we do not lose heart. We have renounced disgraceful, underhanded ways; we refuse to practice cunning or to tamper with God's word, but by the open statement of the truth we would commend ourselves to every man's conscience in the sight of God. And even if our Gospel is veiled, it is veiled only to those who are perishing. In their case the god of this world has blinded

---

3. In this section, I am particularly indebted to G. Quispel, "Hermetism and the New Testament, Especially Paul," in *Aufstieg und Niedergang der römischen Welt* 2.22 (forthcoming).

the minds of the unbelievers, to keep them from seeing the light
of the Gospel of the glory of Christ, who is the likeness of God.
For what we preach is not ourselves, but Jesus Christ as Lord, with
ourselves as your servants for Jesus' sake. For it is the God who
said, "Let light shine out of darkness," who has shone in our hearts
to give the light of the knowledge of the glory of God in the face
of Christ.

Paul ends this passage by identifying the glory of God with Christ. The
question is how literally does he mean it? There is no reason to think that
he is not being fully literal and candid, since it was a sensible expectation
of apocalyptic Jews in the first century. I suggest that he is using these
terms in their biblical technical sense to identify the Christ with the
human manifestation of God.

For now, the main point must be the usually unappreciated use of
the language of transformation in Paul's works. Indeed, as we shall see,
Paul's entire description of resurrection is framed around his visionary
experience, which in turn carries his argument that he is the equal of
the fleshly disciples and apostles of Jesus. In 2 Cor 3:18, Paul says that
believers will be changed into Christ's likeness from one degree of glory
to another. He refers to Exod 33–34, where Moses' encounter with the
angel of the Lord is narrated. Earlier in that passage, the angel of the
Lord is described as carrying the name of God (23:21). Moses sees the
glory of the Lord, makes a covenant, receives the commandments upon
the two tables of the law, and when he comes down from the mount the
skin of his face shines with light (34:29–35). The identification of the
"glory of the Lord" and the "angel of the Lord," God's principal angel, is
a most important aspect of the tradition. It is angelic status that brings
with it immortality.

In any event, in Exodus Moses thereafter must wear a veil except when
he is in the presence of the Lord. Paul assumes that Moses made an ascension to the presence of the Lord, was transformed by that encounter,
and that his shining face is a reflection of the encounter, perhaps even
as a foretaste of his angelic destiny.

So far Paul is using strange and significant mystical language. But what is immediately striking about it is that Paul uses that language to discuss his own and other Christians' experience in Christ. Paul explicitly compares Moses' experience with his own and that of Christian believers. Their transformation is of the same sort, but the Christian transformation is greater and more permanent. Once the background of the vocabulary is pointed out, Paul's daring claims for Christian experience become clear. The point, therefore, is that some Christian believers also make such an ascent somehow and that its effects are more permanent than the vision which Moses received. The church has witnessed a theophany as important as the one vouchsafed to Moses, but the Christian theophany is greater still, as Paul himself has experienced. The Corinthians are said to be a message from Christ (2 Cor 3:2), who is equated with the glory of God. The new community of Gentiles is not a letter written on stone (Jer 31:33), but it is delivered by Paul as Moses delivered the Torah to Israel. The new dispensation is more splendid than the last, not needing the veil with which Moses hid his face. Paul's own experience proved to him and for Christianity that all will be transformed.

Thus, Paul's term *the glory of the Lord* must be taken as both a reference to Christ and a technical term for *kavod,* the human form of God appearing in biblical visions. In 2 Cor 3:18, Paul says that Christians behold the glory of the Lord (*tēn doxan kyriou*) as in a mirror and are transformed into his image (*tēn autēn eikona*).[4] For Paul, as for the ear-

---

4. The use of the mirror here is also a magico-mystical theme, which can be traced to the word *'ayin* in Ezek 1. Although it is sometimes translated otherwise, *'ayin* probably refers to a mirror even there and possibly refers to some unexplained technique for achieving ecstasy. The mystic bowls of the magical papyri and talmudic times were filled with water and oil to reflect light and stimulate trance. The magical papyri describe spells which use a small bowl as the medium for the appearance of a god for divination; e.g., *Papyri Graecae Magicae* 4.154–285 (cf. H. D. Betz, *The Greek Magical Papyri in Translation, Including the Demotic Spells* [2d ed.; Chicago: University of Chicago Press, 1996], 40–43); *Papyri Demoticae Magicae* 14.1–92, 295–308, 395–427, 528–53, 627–35, 805–40, 841–50, 851–55 (Betz, *Greek Magical Papyri,* 195–200, 213, 218–19, 225–26, 229, 236–39). The participant concentrates on the reflection in the water's surface, often with oil added to the mixture, sometimes with the light of a lamp nearby. Lamps and charms are also used to produce divinations, presumably because they can stimulate trance under the proper conditions. The *Reuyoth Yehezkel,* for instance, mention that Ezekiel's mystical vision was stimulated by looking into the waters of the River Chebar. It seems to me that Philo (*Contemplative Life* 78) appropriates the mystic imagery of the mirror to discuss the allegorical exposition of Scripture; see D. Georgi, *Die Gegner des Paulus in 2. Korintherbrief: Studien zur religiosen Propaganda in der Spatantike* (Wissenschaftliche Monographien zum Alten und Neuen Testament 11; Neukirchen-Vluyn: Neukirchener Verlag, 1964), 272–73; S. Schulz, "Die Decke des Moses: Untersuchungen zu einer vorpaulinischen Überlieferung in II Cor. 3:7–18," *Zeitschrift für neutestamentliche Wissenschaft* 49 (1958): 1–30. Paul's opponents then look into the mirror and see only the text. But because Paul and those truly in Christ actually behold the glory of the Lord, they

liest Jewish mystics, to be privileged enough to see the *kavod* or glory (*doxa*) of God is a prologue to transformation into his image (*eikōn*). Paul does not say that all Christians have literally made the journey but compares the experience of knowing Christ to being allowed into the intimate presence of the Lord.

The result of the journey is to identify Christ as the glory of the Lord. When Paul says that he preaches that Jesus is Lord and that God "has let this light shine out of darkness into our hearts to give the light of knowledge of the glory of God in the face of Christ" (2 Cor 4:6), he seems clearly to be describing his own conversion and ministry, just as he described it in Gal 1 and just as he is explaining the experience to new converts for the purpose of furthering conversion. His apostolate, which he expresses as "a prophetic calling," is to proclaim that the face of Christ is the glory of God. It is difficult not to read this passage in terms of Paul's description of the ascension of the man to the third heaven and conclude that Paul's conversion experience also involved his identification of Jesus as the "image" and "glory of God," as the human figure in heaven, and thereafter as Christ, Son, and Savior. Or at least this is how Paul construes it when he recalls it, which is all that anyone can say for sure. But we shall need to revisit this question later.

The identification of Christ with the glory of God brings a transformation and sharing of the believer with the image as well. This is the same as regaining the image of God which Adam lost. This transformation is accomplished through death and rebirth in Christ, which can be experienced in direct visions as Paul apparently did or subsequently by anyone through baptism. Notice, however, how completely the theophanic language from Greek and Jewish mystical piety has been appropriated for discussing what we today call conversion. It is Paul's primary language for describing the experience of conversion because it gives a sense of the transformation and divinizing that he feels is inherent in his encounter with the risen Christ. As we shall see in various texts, this transformation and divinizing is authenticated in communal life and social transactions (e.g., 1 Cor 12–14; 5:1–5).

---

have a clearer vision on the truth. My thanks to David Balch for insisting that I deal with these issues, though he will no doubt dissent from my opinion.

Paul is also contrasting his kind of Christianity with its apocalyptic acceptance of visionary evidence with a Judaism or Jewish Christianity of some sort, a movement which suspected all such experience and concentrated on extending biblical law into ordinary experience. He may have Pharisaism in mind and he may be referring to some of his Jewish-Christian opponents, since there was no clear break between Judaism and Christianity at this time. But the exact identity of his opponents is not important for the moment. The purpose of the analogy is clear: whenever anybody turns to the Lord through Christianity, the veil of Moses is removed. Upon the faces of the new Christians is the reflection of Christ, since they bear the same image as Christ, who as spirit allows the image of God to live among them and with them. I. M. Lewis outlines sharply the effect of such a claim of "spirit possession in society."[5] The Christians were a peripheral group in Jewish society whose claim to have direct access to the truth through the Spirit rendered Pharisaic claims of authoritative exegesis irrelevant.

Ecstatic ascensions like the one described in 2 Cor 12 and spiritual metamorphoses like 2 Cor 3 are strangely unfamiliar to modern Jewish and Christian religious sentiments. Neither Christianity nor rabbinic Judaism openly transmitted these lively mystical Jewish traditions of the first century. But in the context of the first few centuries, the combination of these two themes of ascension and transformation, both inside and outside Judaism, normally suggested the gaining of immortality, and the context of Jewish mysticism also connects with the issue of theodicy. Daniel 12 suggests that those who lead others to wisdom (*hammaskilim,* the enlighteners) will shine as the brightness of the heavens, like the stars, and that they will obviously be among those previously described as resurrected for eternal reward:

> At that time shall arise Michael, the great prince who has charge of your people. And there shall be a time of trouble, such as never has been since there was a nation till that time; but at that time your people shall be delivered, every one whose name shall be found

---

5. I. M. Lewis, *Ecstatic Religion: An Anthropological Study of Spirit Possession and Shamanism* (Baltimore: Penguin, 1971).

written in the book. And many of those who sleep in the dust of the earth shall awake, some to everlasting life, and some to shame and everlasting contempt. And those who are wise shall shine like the brightness of the firmament; and those who turn many to righteousness, like the stars for ever and ever. (Dan 12:1–3)

Besides the general resurrection and punishment, a very interesting special reward is promised to those who make others wise. They shall shine like the brightness of the heaven (*zohar haraqia'*), like or as the stars forever. It is probable that the prophet here means not just a literary figure of speech, but the literal identification of the knowledge-givers with the stars. They shall be luminous beings, shining as stars, which most likely means that they shall become angels because stars had been identified as angelic creatures from earliest times (e.g., Judg 5:20 and Job 38:7). One should also note that the term for brightness in this passage is *zohar*, not accidently the name of the principal work of Kabbalah, the *Zohar*. Early Kabbalah was very interested in Dan 12, which was significantly understood to mean angelic transformation in the Zohar.

The parables of Enoch (1 Enoch 37–71) contain the interesting narration of the transformation of Enoch into the Son of Man, but no one can be sure that this is not a Christian addition to the text, since it agrees so completely with the transformation that Paul outlines.[6] Without Paul we could not suppose that this experience is evidenced in the first century because the date of 1 Enoch is uncertain. Nor would we know that the mystic experience was even possible within Judaism. It seems clear then that the Son of Man in Dan 7:13 is yet another example of the principal manifestation of God who was similarly identified with Christ.

Paul's famous description of Christ's experience of humility and obedience in Phil 2:5–11 also hints that the identification of Jesus with the image of God was reenacted in the church in a liturgical mode:

---

6. The romance of exaltation to immortality was hardly a unique Jewish motif; rather it was characteristic of all higher spirituality of later Hellenism — witness the Hermetic literature. Even in a relatively unsophisticated text like the magical *Recipe for Immortality* (the so-called Mithras Liturgy) of third-century Egypt, the adept gains a measure of immortality by gazing directly on the god and breathing in some of his essence.

Have this mind among yourselves, which is yours in Christ Jesus, who, though he was in the form of God, did not count equality with God a thing to be grasped, but emptied himself, taking the form of a servant, being born in the likeness of humankind. And being found in human form he humbled himself and became obedient unto death, even death on a cross. Therefore God has highly exalted him and bestowed on him the name which is above every name, that at the name of Jesus every knee should bow, in heaven and on earth and under the earth, and every tongue confess that Jesus Christ is Lord, to the glory of God the Father. (Phil 2:5–11)

In Phil 2:6, the identification of Jesus with the "form of God" implies his preexistence. The Christ is depicted as an eternal aspect of divinity which was not proud of its high station but consented to take on the shape of a man and suffer the fate of men, even death on a cross (though many scholars see this phrase as a Pauline addition to the original hymn). This transformation of form from divinity is followed by the converse, the retransformation into God. Because of this obedience God exalted Jesus and bestowed on him the "name which is above every name" (2:9). For a Jew this phrase can only mean that Jesus received the divine name *yhwh,* the tetragrammaton, understood as the Greek name *kyrios* (Lord). We have already seen that sharing in the divine name is a frequent motif of the early Jewish apocalypticism where the principal angelic mediator of God is or carries the name Yahweh, as Exod 23 describes the angel of Yahweh. Indeed the implication of the Greek term *morphē* (form) is that Christ has the form of a divine body identical with the *kavod,* the glory, and equivalent also with the *eikōn,* for humankind is made after the *eikōn* of God and thus has the divine *morphē* (= Hebrew *demuth*). The climax of Paul's confession is that "Jesus Christ is Lord to the glory of God the Father" (Phil 2:11), meaning that Jesus the Messiah has received the name Lord in his glorification and that this name, not Jesus' private earthly name, is the one which will cause every knee to bend and every tongue confess.[7]

---

7. The bibliography on the Pauline and post-Pauline hymns in Phil 2:6–11 and Col 1:15–20 appears endless. See E. Schillebeeckx, *Jesus: An Experiment in Christology* (New York: Seabury, 1979);

In paraphrasing this fragment from liturgy, Paul witnesses that the early Christian community directed its prayers to this human figure of divinity along with God (1 Cor 12:3; 16:22; Rom 10:9–12) — all the more striking since the Christians, like the Jews, refuse to give any other god or hero any veneration at all. When the rabbis gained control of the Jewish community they vociferously argued against the worship of any angel and specifically polemicized against the belief that a heavenly figure other than God can forgive sins (Babylonian Talmud, tractate *Sanhedrin* 38b), quoting Exod 23:21 prominently among other Scriptures to prove their point. The heresy itself they called believing that there are "two powers in heaven." By this term the rabbis largely (but not exclusively) referred to Christians who, as Paul says, did exactly what the rabbis warned against — worship the second power.[8]

Concomitant with Paul's worship of the divine Christ is transformation. Paul says in Phil 3:10 "that I may know him and the power of his resurrection and may share his sufferings, becoming like him in his death (*symmorphizomenos tō thanatō autou*)." Later, in 3:20–21, he says: "But our commonwealth is in heaven, and from it we await a Savior, the Lord Jesus Christ, who will change (*metaschēmatisei*) our lowly body to be conformed in shape (*symmorphon*) to his glorious body (*tō sōmati tēs doxēs autou*) by the power which enables him even to subject all things to himself (*kata tēn energeian tou dynasthai auton kai hypotaxai autō ta panta*)."

English does not allow us to build such a vivid image into one word. If we had an English word for it, it would be *symmorphosize*, like *metamorphosize* but with a more intimate and transformative meaning. The

---

M. Hengel, "Hymn and Christology," *Studia Biblica* 1972: 173–97; repr. in Hengel's *Between Jesus and Paul: Studies in the Earliest History of Christianity* (trans. J. Bowden; Philadelphia: Fortress, 1983), 78–96; J. Murphy O'Connor, "Christological Anthropology in Phil. 2:6–11," *Revue biblique* 83 (1976): 25–50; and D. Georgi, "Der vorpaulinische Hymnus Phil. 2:6–11," in *Zeit und Geschichte: Dankesgabe an Rudolf Bultmann* (ed. E. Dinkler; Tübingen: Mohr, 1964), 263–93, esp. 291 for bibliography. As David Balch reminds me, Käsemann emphasizes that Paul's metaphoric use of the body and its separate parts is characteristic of parenetic sections, emphasizing the relationship between the believer and the risen Lord. See E. Schweitzer, "sw'ma ktl.," in *Theological Dictionary of the New Testament* (ed. G. Kittel and G. Friedrich; trans. G. W. Bromiley; Grand Rapids: Eerdmans, 1971), 7.1073.

8. See my *Two Powers in Heaven: Early Rabbinic Reports about Christianity and Gnosticism* (Leiden: Brill, 1977), 33–158, esp. 68–73; and L. W. Hurtado, "The Binitarian Shape of Early Christian Worship," in *The Jewish Roots of Christological Monotheism: Papers from the St. Andrews Conference on the Historical Origins of the Worship of Jesus* (ed. C. C. Newman et al.; Leiden: Brill, 1999), 187–213.

Greek verb literally means "to be transformed together," what our word *metamorphosize* suggests, except that it states that the reformation will take place together with something else. It is approximately what our children call being "morphed" into another creature. The body of the believer eventually is to be transformed into the body of Christ. The believer's body is to be understood as a body of glory like that of the Savior. And Paul exhorts his followers to imitate him as he has imitated Christ (3:17): "Brethren, join in imitating me, and mark those who so live as you have an example in us (*symmimētai mou ginesthe, adelphoi, kai skopeite tous houtō peripatountas kathōs echete typon hēmas*)." All of this suggests that the body of believers will be literally refashioned into the glorious body of Christ, a process which starts with conversion and faith but ends in the culmination of history, which will shortly be upon us. It all depends on a notion of body which spiritualizes matter, a new body which is not flesh and blood, which cannot inherit the kingdom (1 Cor 15:30).

Paul's depiction of salvation and the transformation of the believer is based on his understanding of Christ's glorification, partaking of early Jewish apocalyptic mysticism for its expression.[9] It may even have survived from a pre-Christian setting because Paul does not mention resurrection here at all. Clearly glorification is doing the job of resurrection in this passage. Likewise, in Rom 12:2 Paul's listeners are exhorted to "be transformed (*metamorphousthe*) by renewing of your minds." In Gal 4:19 Paul expresses another but very similar transformation: "My little children, with whom I am again in travail until Christ be formed in you

---

9. Scholars like Kim who want to ground all of Paul's thought in a single ecstatic conversion experience, which they identify with Luke's accounts of Paul's conversion, are reticent to accept this passage as a fragment from Christian liturgy because to do so would destroy its value as Paul's personal revelatory experience; see S. Kim, *The Origin of Paul's Gospel* (Grand Rapids: Eerdmans, 1982) and *Paul and the New Perspective: Second Thoughts on The Origins of Paul's Gospel* (Grand Rapids: Eerdmans, 2001). But there is no need to decide whether the passage is originally Paul's (hence received directly through the Damascus revelation) since ecstatic language normally is derived from traditions current within the religious group. Christian mystics use Christian language; Muslim mystics use the languages developed for mysticism in Islam; and no mystic is ever confused by another religion's mysticism unless it is the conscious and explicit intent of the mystic's vision to do so. See R. C. Zaehner's, *Hinduism and Muslim Mysticism* (New York: Schocken, 1969); S. Katz, "Language, Epistemology, and Mysticism," in *Mysticism and Philosophical Analysis* (ed. S. Katz; New York: Oxford University Press, 1982), 22–75. In this case the language is not even primarily Christian. The basic language is from Jewish mysticism, though the subsequent exegesis about the identification of the Christ with the figure on the throne is Christian; the vision of God enthroned is the goal of Jewish mystical speculation.

(*mechris ou morphōthē christos en hymin*)!" This transformation is to be effected by being transformed into him in his death (*symmorphizomenos tō thanatō autou;* Phil 3:10). These are crucial issues for understanding Paul's religious experience. They show that he predicts that the believer will be transformed into the glorious body of Christ, through dying and being reborn in Christ. Paul sees the phenomenon as being related to baptism but it is probable that in his own life this realization is related to his own conversion and revelatory life. There is no doubt in my mind that what Paul experienced was the beginning of the fulfillment of the prophecy in Dan 12 that those who are wise shall shine like the brightness of the heaven. Paul felt in his own life this call to be transformed into an angelic creature, a process which has already started but which will find fulfillment in the eschaton, which will be quickly upon us.

Paul's central proclamation is this: Jesus is Lord and all who have faith have already undergone a death like his and so will share in his resurrection by being transformed into his form and shape. This proclamation reflects a baptismal liturgy, implying that baptism provides the moment whereby the believer comes to be "in Christ." Christianity may have been a unique Jewish sect in making baptism a central rather than a preparatory ritual, but some of the mystical imagery comes from its Jewish past.

Alternatively, Paul can say, as he does in Gal 1:16 that "God was pleased to reveal his son in me (*en emoi*)." This is not a simple dative but refers to his having received in him the Spirit, in his case through his conversion. Being in Christ in fact appears to mean being united with or transformed into his heavenly image. The same, however, is available to all Christians through baptism. Dying and being resurrected along with Christ in baptism is the beginning of the process by which the believer gains the same image of God, his *eikōn*, which was made known to humanity when Jesus became the Son of Man — that human figure in heaven who brings judgment in the apocalypse described by Daniel.

Paul's conception of the risen body of Christ as the spiritual body (1 Cor 15:43) at the end of time and as the body of glory (Phil 3:21) thus originates in Jewish apocalypticism and mysticism, modified by the unique events of early Christianity. The meaning of Rom 8:29 can be likewise clarified by Jewish esoteric tradition. There Paul speaks of God as having "foreordained his elect to be conformed to the image of his Son (*symmorphous tēs eikonos tou huiou autou*)." Paul uses the genitive here rather than the dative as in Phil 3:21, softening the identification between believer and Savior. But when Paul states that believers conform to the image of his Son, he is not speaking of an agreement of mind or ideas between Jesus and the believers. Again, the word *symmorphous* itself suggests a spiritual reformation of the believer's body into the form of the divine image. Paul's language for conversion — being in Christ — develops out of mystical Judaism.

This, it seems to me, is the reward that Paul expects Jews to gain when they join Christianity. It may be that Paul assumes all who are part of Israel to be saved, as he says in Romans. What he is offering those who believe in Christ is not merely salvation but transformation. This is beyond the rewards offered by Sadduceeism certainly, and Pharisaism as well, to righteous Jews. He is maintaining that those who believe in Christ, Jew or Gentile alike, will join him in his heavenly body.

Paul speaks of the transformation being partly experienced by believers already in their pre-parousia existence. His use of the present tense in Rom 12:2 and 2 Cor 3:18 underscores that transformation is an ongoing event. However in 1 Cor 15:49 and Rom 8 it culminates at Christ's return, the parousia. This suggests that for Paul transformation is both a single, definitive event, yet also a process that continues until the second coming. The redemptive and transformative process appears to correspond exactly with the turning of the ages. This age is passing away, though it certainly remains a present evil reality (1 Cor 3:19; 5:9; 2 Cor 4:4; Gal 1:4; Rom 12:2). The gospel, which is the power of God for salvation (Rom 1:16), is progressing through the world (Phil 1:12; also Rom 9–11).

Angel Christology in the Gospels

This understanding of Jesus' resurrection body follows from a very striking social organization and striking notions of how to carry on the Christian life. In his fine book *Luke-Acts: Angels, Christology, and So-*

teriology, Crispin H. T. Fletcher-Louis suggests that the phrase *ton nomon eis diatagas angelōn* (usually translated "the law as delivered by angels") in Acts 7:53 may mean something far more important: "a community whose constitution is to live in conformity with (i.e., according to the law of) the angels."[10] If Fletcher-Louis is correct, and his work has been paralleled independently by the fine book by Turid Seim,[11] then the social practice being advocated by the Gospels is one of living as an angel, chastely, while still in the flesh. It also suggests to me that we have misunderstood Paul's statement in Gal 3:19: "Why then the law? It was added because of transgressions, till the offspring should come to whom the promise had been made; and it was ordained by angels through an intermediary (*diatageis di' angelōn en cheiri mesitou*)."

This statement about the giving of Torah is normally translated "it was ordained by angels through an intermediary." But Paul's statement is notoriously difficult because nowhere in Jewish tradition is the law pictured as given through angels; if anything, the opposite is true in rabbinic literature.[12] The midrash and the Passover Haggadah explicitly say that Torah law was given directly by God: "not by an angel, not by a mediator." Perhaps Gal 3:19 also ought to be translated something like "ordained to *conform with the* [*rules of the*] *angels* through the hand of a mediator."

Whether this is explicitly meant at this point, there is no question that something of this nature is indicated in the early Christian preference for celibacy, even as early as Paul.[13] As Fletcher-Louis expresses the conception:

> This is an interpretation which is particularly attractive for a
> number of reasons. Given the thrust of our argument so far we
> have found substantial evidence that for Luke the Christian life

---

10. C. H. T. Fletcher-Louis, *Luke-Acts: Angels, Christology, and Soteriology* (Wissenschaftliche Untersuchungen zum Neuen Testament 2/94; Tübingen: Mohr, 1997), 98–107. See now his *All the Glory of Adam: Liturgical Anthropology in the Dead Sea Scrolls* (Leiden: Brill, 2002).

11. T. K. Seim, *The Double Message: Patterns of Gender in Luke-Acts* (Nashville: Abingdon, 1994).

12. See T. Callan, "The Law and the Mediator: Gal. 3:19b–20" (Ph.D. diss., Yale University, 1976).

13. Seim, *Double Message*, 185–260; see also K. Vogt, "'Becoming Male': A Gnostic and Early Christian Metaphor," in *The Image of God: Gender Models in Judaeo-Christian Tradition* (ed. K. E. Borresen; Minneapolis: Fortress, 1995), 170–86.

could be considered a διαταγή ἀγγέλων. That angelic constitution expresses itself paradigmatically in a life of angelic worship (Lk 15:1–10, cf. 1 Cor 13:1) and a social order in which normal conjugal relations are transcended (Lk 20:34–6). It may not be a complete coincidence that Stephen is introduced at the point where Luke gives us the most concrete and extensive evidence of Christian widows in his two volume work (Acts 6:1ff). Stephen is responsible for a Christian welfare system for those unmarried. Given our reading of Lk 20:34–38, that system is predicated on the relativisation of the levirate law and the attainment of the angelomorphic life. From the point of view of those who charge that Stephen had "blasphemed Moses," that he uttered "words against...the Torah," and that Jesus would "change the customs which Moses handed down" (Acts 6:11, 13–14), this may have had something to do with the relativisation of the levirate law by this early Christian community. From the point of view of the Lukan Stephen his accusers should have looked no further for the fulfillment of the Torah's desire to construct a διαταγή ἀγγέλων than the community described in Acts 6, who live in fulfillment of Lk 20:34–36. Stephen's own angelic appearance (Acts 6:15) should have alerted them to the fact that Torah's intention was now fulfilled in the Christian community.[14]

Envisioning early Christian life, especially in its sexual aspects, as the life of angels is a significant part of Luke's portrayal of the early community:

> And Jesus said to them, "The sons of this age marry and are given in marriage; but those who are accounted worthy to attain to that age and to the resurrection from the dead neither marry nor are given in marriage, for they cannot die any more, because they are equal to angels and are sons of God, being sons of the resurrection." (Luke 20:34–36)

It further suggests that celibacy is a sure way to attain the status of

---

14. Fletcher-Lewis, *Luke-Acts*, 103.

angels, and having attained that status they are already immortal because they are the equivalents of the angels, even called sons of God.
It certainly attains to the status that Paul suggested was implicit in baptism, a status not only surpassing the slave/free and the Jew/Gentile
distinction but also transcending the male/female distinction. And, as
Fletcher-Louis points out, this is the state in which Paul lived and the
one that he recommended rather than marriage:

> Only, let every one lead the life which the Lord has assigned to him,
> and in which God has called him. This is my rule in all the churches.
> Was any one at the time of his call already circumcised? Let him
> not seek to remove the marks of circumcision. Was any one at the
> time of his call uncircumcised? Let him not seek circumcision. For
> neither circumcision counts for anything nor uncircumcision, but
> keeping the commandments of God. Every one should remain in
> the state in which he was called. Were you a slave when called?
> Never mind. But if you can gain your freedom, avail yourself of
> the opportunity. For he who was called in the Lord as a slave is a
> freedman of the Lord. Likewise he who was free when called is a
> slave of Christ. You were bought with a price; do not become slaves
> of men. So, brethren, in whatever state each was called, there let
> him remain with God. Now concerning the unmarried, I have no
> command of the Lord, but I give my opinion as one who by the
> Lord's mercy is trustworthy. I think that in view of the present
> distress it is well for a person to remain as he is. Are you bound to
> a wife? Do not seek to be free. Are you free from a wife? Do not
> seek marriage. But if you marry, you do not sin, and if a girl marries
> she does not sin. Yet those who marry will have worldly troubles,
> and I would spare you that. I mean, brethren, the appointed time
> has grown very short; from now on, let those who have wives live
> as though they had none, and those who mourn as though they
> were not mourning, and those who rejoice as though they were
> not rejoicing, and those who buy as though they had no goods,
> and those who deal with the world as though they had no dealings
> with it. For the form of this world is passing away. I want you to

be free from anxieties. The unmarried man is anxious about the affairs of the Lord, how to please the Lord; but the married man is anxious about worldly affairs, how to please his wife, and his interests are divided. And the unmarried woman or girl is anxious about the affairs of the Lord, how to be holy in body and spirit; but the married woman is anxious about worldly affairs, how to please her husband. (1 Cor 7:17–34)

In this passage, Paul suggests that the baptismal formula is to be treated as a prescription for behavior as much as possible. People can remain in the state that they are, not seeking to be circumcised, for example. If one is a slave, there is little to be done, except to take opportunities for freedom if they are legally offered. In the case of the Jew/Gentile distinction, one should not take explicit steps to change one's status. The same in the case of marriage. Married men should remain in their married state, but single men should not seek to marry. Married couples are anxious about their "worldly" affairs and so cannot concentrate as well on the affairs of the Lord. It seems to me that this is the meaning of the famous baptismal formula: "There is neither Jew nor Greek, there is neither slave nor free, there is neither male nor female; for you are all one in Christ Jesus" (Gal 3:28); or, "For there is no distinction between Jew and Greek; the same Lord is Lord of all and bestows his riches upon all who call upon him" (Rom 10:12). Paul has not the present in mind so much as the eschatological end. But by living like angels without these distinctions being relevant, one participates in the coming eschaton, perhaps even forces its presence among us.

This prescription and the equivalent statements in Luke-Acts suggest, as Fletcher-Louis and Seim state, that the status of angels (Fletcher-Louis's term is "angelomorphism") was attained by a holy life and by practicing sexual celibacy, in effect, transcending one's sexual role in life. This imitates the state of the angels and, in Paul's considered opinion, is part of the transformation (*symmorphōsis*) process which will culminate in the coming eschaton. The notion of the importance of celibacy and the possibility of divinization or *apotheōsis* in Greek is clearly present in the writings of the Dead Sea Scrolls, Josephus's description of the Essenes,

Philo's description of a group of Jewish mystics he knows and calls the
Therapeutai (the healers), the Jewish Apocrypha, and occasionally also
in rabbinic literature.[15] Clearly, everyone wished to attain the status
of angels and thought that a righteous life would help to do so. The
question is: what else was necessary?

The resurrection appearances of the Gospels are neither a very great
quantity of material nor do they in any significant way parallel Paul's
statements of the various people to whom Jesus appeared. Paul speaks
of a formulaic set of appearances in which he figures as the last but least
and most modest member. But the Gospels have a considerably more
ramified tradition that does not intersect with Paul in very many ways.[16]

2 Corinthians 12

The result therefore is to see both a deep similarity and continuity between Paul, Peter, and the Gospels and also some significant differences,
as Goulder suggests. The love that Paul has in mind that is greater than
even talking in tongues is an angelic love for we shall all be changed into
angels and love each other chastely and speak to each other in angelic
tongues. And this seems to be the vision which the Gospels share as well,
though they may have a very different view of Jesus' resurrection. With
all these points, Goulder and I are in substantial agreement. Indeed, he
is a very important partisan of the idea that Jewish mystical ascents are
at issue in 2 Cor 12. The difficulty between us is whether Paul is in favor
of them. He is surely trying to argue that his opponents have arrogated
too much authority from their charismatic gifts.

The largest difficulty between Goulder and me comes in how to
understand what is being claimed by Paul in 2 Cor 12:

> I must boast; there is nothing to be gained by it, but I will go on
> to visions and revelations of the Lord. I know a man in Christ who
> fourteen years ago was caught up to the third heaven — whether

---

15. See ibid., passim; and the forthcoming dissertation by Jonah Steinberg.

16. See C. F. Evans, *Resurrection and the New Testament* (London: SCM, 1970), 52, 128; P. Carnley,
The Structure of Resurrection Belief (Oxford: Clarendon, 1987), 18; G. J. Riley, *Resurrection Reconsidered:
Thomas and John in Controversy* (Minneapolis: Fortress, 1995), 88–89 and n. 64.

in the body or out of the body, I do not know, God knows. And I know that this man was caught up into paradise — whether in the body or out of the body, I do not know, God knows — and he heard things that cannot be told, which many may not utter. On behalf of this man, I will boast, but on my own behalf I will not boast, except of my weaknesses. Though if I wish to boast, I shall not be a fool, for I shall be speaking the truth. But I refrain from it so that no one may think more of me than he sees in me or hears from me. And to keep me from being too elated by the abundance of revelations, a thorn was given me in the flesh, a messenger of Satan, to harass me, to keep me from being too elated. Three times I besought the Lord about this, that it should leave me; but he said to me, "My grace is sufficient for you, for my power is made perfect in weakness." (2 Cor 12:1–9)

Goulder sees Paul as countering the easy claims of the Petrines with claims to special spiritual revelations. He sees the ascent to be taken by a close friend, about whom Paul is boasting.[17] I see a great likelihood that Paul is actually talking about himself and making claim to an ascent, about which he will not boast in this context.[18] It is not as clear to me as it is to Goulder that it is Petrines who are making these claims. But that is not significant at the moment. What is significant is that Paul is saying quite overtly that his own claims for spiritual gifts go far beyond anything that his opponents can claim with speaking in tongues and such phenomena. I take it we are in agreement about these issues.

In two articles Goulder goes into more detail.[19] Here is where we most disagree. For his interpretation to work properly, vision (*optasia*) must denote heavenly journey explicitly and not merely any vision. John must have the same Petrine opponents in mind as Paul (and they must be "halakic" opponents), since Paul appears to deny that he has seen God (certainly John 1:18 and 1 John 4:12 deny that anyone has seen God).

---

17. Goulder, *Tale of Two Missions*, 49.

18. A. F. Segal, *Paul the Convert: The Apostolate and Apostasy of Saul the Pharisee* (New Haven: Yale University Press, 1990), 35.

19. M. D. Goulder, "Vision and Knowledge," *Journal for the Study of the New Testament* 56 (1994): 53–71; idem, "The Visionaries of Laodicea," *Journal for the Study of the New Testament* 43 (1991): 15–39.

Lastly, the description of the heavenly journey in 2 Cor 12 must then be a kind of deliberate and ferocious parody of ascent mysticism. But I cannot agree with these statements. *Optasia* seems to me to be any kind of vision; Paul and John may have the same opponents in mind, but some of the opponents in John do not appear to me to be especially halakic in their approach to Christian opposition in that they are persecuting Christians. Furthermore, *merkabah* mysticism never claimed to have seen God, only the angels of God and, in particular, God's principal angel enthroned in heaven, a figure known by a number of names but principally Son of Man in Christianity, with whom Jesus has been identified. The discussion must, I think, remain open on a number of points.

Goulder's main point must be, and with this I agree, that Paul disapproved of the abuse of such visions to manipulate the churches. But the demonstration of these passages (Colossians and Ephesians, as well as the Gospel of John and Revelation) seem to me to come from later times. Paul himself could be "backhandedly" bragging of his own experience: "On behalf of this man I will boast, but on my own behalf I will not boast, except of my weaknesses" (2 Cor 12:5). The change of person from third to first gives me the clear impression that Paul is speaking of himself and the context makes this rhetoric understandable. He is arguing for ordinary prayer over glossolia, but if spiritual gifts grant authority, his gifts go far beyond theirs. If so, he obviously is not against the spiritual experience itself, as Goulder says. He is just against using it to legitimize.

Paul certainly supports the notion that Christians have received gifts of the Spirit, some much greater than those claimed by his opponents. Paul is certainly using heavy rhetoric and a touch of irony. But there is no irony in this description of the heavenly gift of ascent. Either he praises his own or another's spiritual ascent. He does not satirize it as silly or ridiculous. Indeed, his argument depends on our understanding that these gifts are far greater than those of the opponents. It is the modern world, wishing to further denounce spiritual gifts, which sees in this passage a satire of ascent. That part of the irony is in our minds, not in Paul's.

SEVEN

PERSONAL REFLECTIONS ON THE GOULDER SYMPOSIUM

An Afterword

Krister Stendahl

I have been asked to present a summary and conclusion of the essays presented at the Goulder symposium. Michael Goulder had to wait a long time and come a long way for this celebration of his studies by colleagues who take him seriously. And the venue is so right. In my mind, Johns Hopkins University is indelibly connected with the name of William Foxwell Albright, a truly creative scholar and independent thinker. When I listen or read Goulder's scholarship, I cannot help remembering a conversation I once had in Oxford in the 1960s. I asked one of his compatriots in our field whether there had been any new ideas in British New Testament scholarship over that last twenty-five years. His answer was: "Heavens, No!" It seems to me that British scholarship often excels in presenting what is well proven and can be said safely — and does it with admirable eloquence. Goulder is the odd man out, and many of us have squirmed from time to time when he challenged our guild to the hilt. That is his specialty and these essays tell him how fruitful, delightful, and meaningful a stimulus that has been.

The word *midrash* can be described as an often edifying interpretation of a text, now opened up into a creative act by playing skillfully on various passages and motifs, often combining them in a most fascinating and scintillating manner. I am reminded of Dominic Crossan's understanding of the passion story as created out of Old Testament texts understood as prophecies.[1] Yet, I prefer the quite different perspective of Paul Van Buren in his last book, published shortly after his death, *According to the Scriptures.*[2] He takes his point of departure in that very phrase as it occurs in the Pauline summary of the faith in 1 Cor 15, and in Van Buren's view the phrase should not be understood as a reference to prooftexts or anxious apologetic arguments. Rather it points to the more organic way in which the Scriptures were what guided the disciples as they tried to understand and express their experiences. What else did they have for processing, as we say today, what they saw, heard, and felt?

Moreover, there is much in Goulder's work that could be understood as a new form of classical typology. Typology can exist without supersessionism — what I rather like to call replacement theology. Typology is to be handled with care. Classical typology was used to trump the old by the new. It is a mighty motif not only in the New Testament, but also in the Old Testament. As Jon Levenson states in his daring book *The Death and Resurrection of the Beloved Son:* "Nowhere does Christianity betray its indebtedness to Judaism more than in its supersessionism."[3] It is Abel over Cain, Isaac over Ishmael, Jacob over Esau, Joseph over his older brothers, and it is Israel over Canaan — and then there is the church and Christianity as the new Israel over synagogue and Judaism. But there is another possibility. I like to call it the gentle, tender typology. There is shape to God's ways to act with the world and the people. The mystery of Passover and the mystery of Easter have symmetry, a common shape. To discern it enriches the understanding. Such a nontrumping gentle typology is the more important for us Gentiles, as we desire a healing of Jewish-Christian relations.

Goulder's essay brings me back to the early 1950s when I came across Philip Carrington's lectionary musings about the paragraph indicators in ancient uncials.[4] I worked along those lines for a while, but then came

---

1. See, for example, J. D. Crossan, *The Cross That Spoke: The Origin of the Passion Narrative* (San Francisco: Harper & Row, 1988).

2. P. M. Van Buren, *According to the Scriptures: The Origins of the Gospel and of the Church's Old Testament* (Grand Rapids: Eerdmans, 1998).

3. J. D. Levenson, *The Death and Resurrection of the Beloved Son: The Transformation of Child Sacrifice in Judaism and Christianity* (New Haven: Yale University Press, 1993), x.

4. See, e.g., P. Carrington, *The Primitive Christian Calendar: A Study in the Making of the Marcan Gospel* (Cambridge: Cambridge University Press, 1952).

to the idea of a catechism structure of Matthew, somewhat analogous to the *Derek Eretz* literature, the *Didache,* and not least the *Manual of Discipline* from Qumran. I could have asked myself if it was my Lutheran genes that caused us to part ways. Lutheran scholar Alfred Seeberg's *Der Katechismus der Urchristenheit* and his other writings were a major factor.[5] It is to be expected that Anglicans should see liturgy and lectionaries everywhere and Lutherans find that "im Anfang war der Katechismus." But I do not think so. I have always been a liturgy and lectionary buff. And those "sections and lections" haunt me still, not least when I listen to Goulder. Furthermore, it should be stated that Goulder's work is full of striking observations, some related to or triggered by his overarching theories, others just fruits of his keen eye. In either case they stick in our minds. I think many of his observations will outlast some of his theories and engender new constructions.

It seems to me that what Bruce Chilton does is show in a striking manner how feasts and their rhythm played in the minds not only of the evangelists, but of all the New Testament writers. I would also like to call attention to the way he reminds us of what I find so especially fascinating with the Matthean Gospel: It is the most Jewish of the four Gospels in the canon, and yet it ends on the note: "Now is Gentile time." The mission discourse command "only to Israel" has its intensified echo in the encounter with the Canaanite mother (Matt 15:21–23). The refusal of power in the temptation story is reversed in the end of the Gospel by the majestic "to me is given all power (*pasa exousia*) in heaven and on earth" and the charge to go to all the Gentiles (*panta ta ethne*) (28:18–20). It is intriguing to speculate about how the Gentiles in Matthew's church — for I think there were many — felt when they heard Jesus saying: "One does not take the bread from the children and give it to the dogs" (Matt 15:21–28; Mark 7:24–30). Actually, I think they enjoyed the woman's clever repartee, and they felt sort of proud. It was one of their own, a Gentile, that made Jesus change his mind — like God had changed his in the story about the prophet Jonah. By the way, there were no Canaanites around in Jesus' time. Matthew uses the word

---

5. A. Seeberg, *Der Katechismus der Urchristenheit* (Leipzig: Deichert, 1903).

as a code word for "utterly Gentile" so that we understand that it is a story to make a point. Rabbis taught by telling such stories about their masters.

With John Kloppenborg at the reins, that scholarly juggernaut called Q seems to be a little more humbly constructed. To use the terms of the Synoptic trade, there were hardly ever "minor agreements" between him and Goulder, but the process of "Gospel making" becomes less mechanical and almost humanized in Kloppenborg's essay.

Robert Derrenbacker brings us to very tangible things — specifically he brings Goulder's construction "to its knees." It is both enjoyable and helpful to picture "hands on" how those holy writers actually did their writing — if they did not dictate as did Paul. As we must move to more complex and organic views of how these wonderful things happened, Derrenbacker's caveat will stick in my mind: Consider the lap of a scribe before the laptop.

Gary Gilbert gives an intriguing presentation where the list of people in Peter's speech on Pentecost (Acts 2) was elucidated by as different phenomena as the archeology of the *sebasteion* at Aphrodisias and the list of the sons of Noah in Gen 10 where there is special mention of their respective languages ("tongues"). I always like it when archeology and texts come together, and that in one scholar.

Speaking of geography, allow me an addendum on Luke's function as the travel agent of the early Christian story. The structure of his Gospel takes us from Galilee to Jerusalem — hence the long travel account peculiar to him (Luke 9:51–18:14) and the way his final chapter refers to Galilee. Mark and Matthew have the women being told that Jesus will meet the male disciples in Galilee. But in Luke we read: "Remember how he told you about his suffering and resurrection *while he was still in Galilee*" (24:6). The story has to end in Jerusalem. In the same manner, the structure of Acts takes us from Jerusalem to Rome. The force of that structure is often obscured by the traditional description of Paul's "three plus one" journeys, traced on the maps at the end of most Bibles. But the syntax — even in the translations — in Acts 18:22–23 hardly indicates that Luke thought of this as the end of one and beginning of another missionary enterprise. What mattered to him is from Jerusalem to Rome.

Another indication of that perspective is the often-overlooked fact that in Acts the name change from Saulos to Paulos is not related to the Damascus experience. Rather, it happens at Paul's first encounter with a Roman official, a proconsul by the name of Sergios Paulos: "But Saulos, who also was Paulos" (13:9). From then on Luke uses only the name Paul — except in the retellings of the Damascus event where the Lord speaks Hebrew, retained in the Greek as *Saoul* (9:4; 22:7; 26:14). The point is the transition from Jerusalem to Rome. I guess that structure also accounts for the "unsatisfactory" end of Acts. Why are we not told what happened to Paul? That was not the point. The point was: from Jerusalem to Rome.

Alan Segal discusses the transformation and the joyous seriousness with which early Christians strove toward angelic life. This not least in the sense that Jesus refers to: "They neither marry nor are they given in marriage" (Mark 12:35; Matt 22:30). Alan challenges us not to downplay the pervasive strength of that drive. After all, for Paul celibacy was the "natural" state for a Christian, and marriage was a concession (1 Cor 7). "Nature" could be transformed. Transformation was a great theme, often lost in my Lutheran tradition. It has been said that in the Catholic, as in the Orthodox tradition, grace is a sunshine that gives you a suntan, but in Lutheran theology it is the strobe light of ever repeated moments of forgiveness. Alan gives me new courage to seek the sunshine — provided the ozone layer is intact.

One element in midrash and in the Jewish tradition of study, teaching, and preaching is certainly the humor. And a Goulder symposium calls for lifting up that liberating element. Did you notice that Goulder could hardly give an answer without giving it a humorous twist? I sometimes lecture on the theme "Jewish Humor from Jesus to Woody Allen." It is easy to hear and see the rabbi's intellectual joy in the humor of many a secularized Jew. The rabbinic habit of teaching by stories told with playfulness bespeaks an awareness that it would be arrogant to try to match the seriousness of the subject. The parables of Jesus have that same twist. I wish we could see, and had not lost, the glint of humor in Jesus' eyes when he told his stories, his parables. After all, not even the most ascetic camel can get through the eye of a needle. The proof for our loss of humor is no doubt found in those commentaries that tell us about the narrow gates called the "eye of a needle" (Matt 19:24; Mark 10:25; Luke 18:25). I am sure there were, but such need to "rescue" the Bible is pathetic. I guess a shepherd who left the ninety-nine in the wilderness and ran after one would be fired, if found out (Matt 18:12; Luke 15:4). And Jesus decided to make the dishonest steward an icon for decisive faith (16:1–9).

Let me end with a quote from Goulder's own presentation:

> This is the sort of hypothesis which would have delighted Karl Popper, the philosopher of science. Popper said that vague or elastic hypotheses were unhelpful, because they could not be proved wrong — they were unfalsifiable. A useful hypothesis was one which involved predictions which could be found false. The more elaborate the hypothesis the better: a very elaborate hypothesis, sometimes called a baroque hypothesis, could be quickly falsified if it were wrong. On such an account, mine is a baroque hypothesis.

Here a baroque hypothesis is one capable of falsification — and hence one with honest vulnerability. It eschews obfuscation, as we say at Harvard. Some people have found Goulder's hypotheses "baroque" in a more common and pejorative sense. But I would like to conclude our symposium by reminding us of the etymology of the word *baroque,* a loan from Portuguese, where *barroco* is a pearl, not quite perfectly rounded, but a real pearl. Goulder's proposal may not be a perfect pearl, but is a pearl nonetheless.

MICHAEL GOULDER
RESPONDS

Many years ago, I had come to the conclusion that Matthew's Gospel was a kind of expanded second edition of Mark, without the need for assuming lost sources. For instance, Mark had a short parable, the seed growing secretly, which Matthew lacks; but instead Matthew has the much more impressive parable of the tares. Instead of supposing that the tares was an independent parable, it is better to see it as his elaboration of the same basic idea. So I was moving beyond the type/antitype idea; and I would never be able to persuade scholars that this was right unless I could show that Jewish writers did the same.

So in the late 1960s, I studied the Books of Chronicles against the earlier form of Israelite history in Samuel-Kings. To my delight, I found that the Chronicler was doing just what I thought Matthew was doing. A famous instance was David's purchase of the temple site. Samuel said that the Lord incited David to number Israel, so causing the plague, and that David paid fifty shekels of silver for the site. Chronicles says that Satan incited David to number Israel and that he paid six hundred shekels of gold. Explanation was not difficult. It was scandalous for God to incite David to sin; and silver was nothing in the days of Solomon — he would have paid gold for so precious a piece of land, and fifty shekels per tribe.

The more I read Chronicles — and other later Jewish literature — the more obvious it became that later writers were editing earlier works, often expanding them in the light of other biblical material; and twice reference is made to such work being found "in the *midrash* of the seer/ prophet Iddo" (2 Chr 12:15; 13:22). Wilhelm Rudolph defined *midrash*

as an edifying reworking of an earlier text; and that is just what I
took Matthew to be.[1] I therefore called my book *Midrash and Lection
in Matthew.*

This seemed a clever move, but it caused much trouble. The word
midrash means inquiry (from the Hebrew verb *darash*, to inquire), and
the Chronicler uses it in the same way that the Greeks used the word
historia, which also means inquiry. I intended the word in the same sense
that the Chronicler used it, and said so. But words change their meaning
with time, and in the Christian era the Jewish community used the word
to mean a commentary on Scripture. Thus I have on my shelves a whole
row of books, the *Midrash Rabbah*, which is an enormous collection of
discussions by the rabbis over hundreds of years on the meaning of the
biblical text. The Chronicler wrote about 350 B.C.E.; so it was easy to
say that I was using the word in a peculiar sense. Jewish scholars are not
in doubt that their community retold Bible stories in expanded forms,
drawing inspiration from other biblical passages: it is just that they tend
to use more general words for this like *exegesis.* The adjective *midrashic* is
often acceptable, as in "a *midrashic* expansion." I have ultimately learned
to be wary of the term *midrash,* because many people do not understand
it, and because think that I do not understand it!

Response to Bruce Chilton

Bruce Chilton writes a characteristically generous, charming, and re-
vealing appreciation of my work. A Cambridge scholar once said to me,
"There have been various views of your book in Cambridge, but Daube
approved of it"; the menace was softened by the mention of Daube, a
polymath Jew. So Chilton's account was not a total shock.

Midrash and Lection in Matthew was my first full-length book, and
it was triply scandalous. First, it disputed the existence of Q, the supposed source known to Luke and Matthew; on this point I was told at
the time that I was *contra mundum.* Second, I suggested that Matthew
was an elaboration, a midrashic expansion, of Mark, as the Books of

---

1. W. Rudolph, *Chronikbücher* (Handbuch zum Alten Testament; Tübingen, Mohr, 1955).

Chronicles were expansions of Samuel-Kings. This was unwelcome in a community which regarded the Q sayings as the best source we have of Jesus' historical teaching (C. H. Dodd's *The Founder of Christianity* had just appeared).[2] Third was the lectionary theory, of which an implausible version by Aileen Guilding had fallen under just criticism.[3] It took Chilton's clear head and independent character to see good in the book in such an atmosphere.

It is intoxicating to think up a radically new approach to the Gospels, and my first account in that book shows some distressing signs of drunkenness. I made three serious mistakes. The Jewish calendar follows two quite different lectionary cycles, a festal and a Sabbath cycle. The evidence for a festal cycle goes back deep into the Old Testament, and it is this cycle that I have followed to this day, as may be seen in my essay in this volume. There is also a Sabbath-by-Sabbath cycle, for which the earliest clear evidence is in the third century of our era; so Morris was justified in saying that the theory is rather speculative here. Worse, although I had a mention of Abel in the first week, Noah in the second, and Abraham in the third, as the Sabbath cycle has, many of the other units had only a distant relation to the supposed Old Testament readings. A third error was to go to the manuscripts for help. I had divided Matthew into some sixty-five units, but feared these would be called speculative; when I found that Codex Alexandrinus divided the Gospel into sixty-nine sections, I leapt to the conclusion that I had support from one of the earliest of our texts. It has taken years for me to see these three mistakes in their full horror. Cambridge scholars were right to suspect the proposal, though they were wrong to miss its possibilities.

I think Chilton is probably right in sensing some theological bias against a locus in worship for the Gospels. People have often said to me that Paul is critical of Jewish feasts; but Luke refers quite naturally to Passover, Pentecost, and "the fast" (Atonement) in Acts, and he was a Gentile. It surely would be automatic for Jewish Christians to continue Jewish worship patterns; only Paul is anxious not to have anything forced on his Gentile converts. Chilton is also right in thinking that

---

2. C. H. Dodd, *The Founder of Christianity* (New York: Macmillan, 1970).
3. A. Guilding, *The Fourth Gospel and Jewish Worship* (Oxford: Clarendon, 1960).

so perfect a cycle as Matthew has provided is no first attempt; I have offered an account of how Mark constitutes an earlier try at a six-and-a-half-month program (*LNP*, chap. 5); and *LNP* proposes a lectionary account of Luke also.

Chilton makes a number of interesting suggestions of alternative lectionary possibilities, and these need to be mulled over. Sometimes they can be combined with my own theory; for instance, Pentecost was a celebration of the vision of God by Moses and Ezekiel, as well as of the giving of the law. I have set it for the beginning of Matt 5, where Jesus goes up on the mountain and says, "Blessed are the pure in heart, for they shall see God." More often we compete: I have the transfiguration story for Dedication because the descent of the cloud of glory is the central moment of Dedication (2 Macc 2:8); but perhaps it was also sometimes told at Tabernacles. It is the nature of a developing liturgy for different things to be tried in different places. My only advantage in principle over Chilton.is that my proposals follow the Jewish festal year in sequence, with the right number of units for the intervening Saturday nights. To me has fallen the humble task of expounding the present text of Matthew; to Chilton the higher vocation of piercing the curtain to what went on before.

Response to John Kloppenborg

John Kloppenborg raises many interesting questions in his high-level essay, and I can comment here only on his central theme: how are we to choose between competing solutions to the Synoptic Problem?

I invoked Karl Popper and Thomas Kuhn in my discussion of this problem in *LNP*, but of course they are both dealing with the logic of scientific discovery. Their language and methods are bound to be applied in a slightly different sense when historical questions are at issue. Furthermore Kuhn's own use of the term *paradigm* is not univocal, and Margaret Masterman singles out a number of different uses in Kuhn's book.[4] My own use of Kuhn is not, however, rhetorical in the sense of

---

4. M. Masterman, "The Nature of a Paradigm," in *Criticism and the Growth of Knowledge* (ed.

vapid. Kuhn is pointing to the way in which a whole array of hypotheses and presuppositions come to dominate a field of study, and Kloppenborg's instance of Reimarus as initiating a shift of paradigm is to the point. Now it may suitably be said that Reimarus's achievement is in a different league from anything I might aspire to; but this does not affect the point. In the more limited field of the relation of the Gospel traditions to the historical Jesus and to one another, we have inherited a cluster of hypotheses and presuppositions which may form the basis of any study without further discussion. The early churches treasured sayings and stories of Jesus; one collection of such sayings and stories, known to us as Q, was available to Matthew and Luke; Matthew and Luke also had access to other collections of material, which we call M and L; Thomas preserves some sayings in an early form; and so on. I claimed to be offering a new paradigm because I dispute this whole established structure of assumption and present an alternative.

Kloppenborg suitably refers to Kuhn's observation that a new paradigm will require the use of new tools; and my proposals have, in an analogous way, involved the study of areas not normally felt relevant. The suggestion that Matthew and Luke created much of the new material themselves meant an inquiry into Jewish methods of retelling a sacred story, and so an examination of the methods of the Chronicler, or of the authors of the Testaments, or of pseudo-Philo. It also meant picking out those features which were characteristic of Luke and Matthew outside their vocabulary: the way Matthew's parables mirror rabbinic parables, for instance, in a way that Luke's do not (I listed thirty ways in which Luke had a style of his own). My theory that the Synoptic Gospels were intended to be read in sections throughout the year needed support from both Jewish and Christian liturgical studies. It is not important to me whether my combined hypotheses deserve the coveted label *new paradigm;* what is important is that it is a challenge to established positions on a broad front. I maintain that seven of the eight standard conclusions are in error.

A significant element in Kloppenborg's argument is the claim to parity for his hypothesis and mine. In one sense this is welcome, because until

---

I. Lakatos and A. Musgrave; Proceedings of the International Colloquium in the Philosophy of Science 4; Cambridge: Cambridge University Press, 1970), 59–89.

recently it could be assumed (as in his citation from Marxsen) that the 2DH was an established conclusion. But, although this is conceded to have been overconfident, it is not the case that the 2DH and the FGH are on all fours. Occam's Razor is a vital principle of inquiry in all fields and is used by Gospel scholars in other contexts: hypotheses should not be multiplied beyond what is necessary. I elaborated Austin Farrer's hypothesis that Luke can be explained as a reworking of Mark and Matthew, three documents of which we believe ourselves to have tolerably exact copies. The 2DH invokes the supposed existence of a fourth document Q: it needs therefore, on Occam's principle, to show that Q is necessary; or in other words that the FGH is in error. My hypothesis has priority of consideration and should be accepted unless it can be shown to be implausible.

Kloppenborg's argument here is sophistical. I had written, "Luke's use of Mark is a fact (or generally accepted as one)," and he criticizes this as a rhetorical flourish, insisting that it is a postulate, just like Q. Of course if we are strict enough, there are no historical facts, because evidence of the past is always limited and something new might turn up and show we had been wrong. Nevertheless, it would be entirely reasonable to say: "It is a fact (or a generally accepted one) that Lee Oswald shot President Kennedy" — although there may be cranks who think he was shot by Lyndon Johnson. I use this rhetorical flourish because I believe, in line with the preponderance of Gospel scholars, that Luke used Mark and that it is possible (and normal) to explain every word of Luke's Markan material on this basis. Q, on the other hand, is merely an unnecessary postulate because (I am arguing) it is possible to explain the Q material as Luke's uses of Matthew. Kloppenborg just muddies the waters when he says, "Q is not a 'mere' postulate; on the contrary, it follows *necessarily* from the two logically prior postulates." But one of these postulates, that Matthew and Luke were independent, is argued to be false! So there is no necessity about it.

Regarding the issue of falsification, I made use of Popper's theory, with its stress on falsification, because of the "soft-liners." There are some problems for the 2DH in the minor agreements in the passion narrative, and it is possible to escape these problems by supposing different editions of Mark, or oral tradition, or multiple sources, or Luke's use of both Matthew and Q. I wished to stress that if one were flexible enough, it would never be possible to know the truth. I respect Schmid and Neirynck and Tuckett (and now Kloppenborg) because they are "hard-liners": they offer a single explanation that Matthew and Luke sometimes agree by coincidence in their independent changes to Mark. This theory can be assessed for plausibility and so tested. I gave the example of the passage where the soldiers blindfold Jesus in Mark, hit him, and say, "Prophesy!"; Matthew and Luke both add the same five words: "Who is it who smote you?" and the word for smote is rare.

Sometimes a single difficulty is striking enough to bring a hypothesis down. I once attended a lecture on the Qumran community, whom the speaker alleged to be "monks, wanting to be alone with God." Someone asked about a note on the handout map indicating the burial place of thirty-seven women and children; and she replied, "That is difficult. Perhaps they were passing through, or helping with the cooking"! I am not so simple as to think that I can persuade the scholarly community to desert the 2DH with a single difficulty, and in an early article, "On Putting Q to the Test," I listed twelve problem passages, seven of which are conceded by Kloppenborg to be difficult. The question then becomes, "How many anomalies are needed to cause a shift of paradigm?"

Kloppenborg's own defense, like Neirynck's, is to point to the unreli-ability of early manuscripts. It is certainly true that a copyist might make an error or perhaps add a phrase familiar from another Gospel. But the trouble is that we have so many families of manuscripts, and the sup-posed original text of Matt 26, without "who is it who smote you?," has not survived in any of them. Thus Matthew wrote autograph A, which was copied by B, C, and D, and B was copied by E, F, and G, and so on. Let us suppose that the addition was made as soon as possible, that is, that it was written by a copyist from his memory of the phrase in Luke within weeks of Luke's being published. Luke is usually thought to have been written some ten years after Matthew; so the only form of Matthew to have survived is from copies of that erroneous form of the text, and all the copies of copies taken from A, B, and C, etc., have disappeared. Most scholars think that pretty unlikely.

I always attacked the 2DH for two weaknesses, one of which was the minor agreements. The other is the extent of vocabulary common to Matthew and Q. The second argument has taken time to clarify in my mind, and Kloppenborg has missed the point of its final form, although he mentions the article where it is set out: "Self-Contradiction in the IQP?"[5] Q scholars are trying to set out what they suppose to have been the version of Q used by Matthew and Luke. About half of the 3,600-odd words in Q are identical in the two Gospels (QC = common words), while half are different (QD). The Q scholar just copies out the QC words, but he has to choose over the QD words. For instance, Matthew often writes "the kingdom of heaven" or "our Father in heaven," and Luke never uses either of these expressions, preferring "the kingdom of God" and "Father." The rule followed is then to suppose that Matthew altered the Q form, which we have in Luke, to fit his special characteristic phrasing; or in other words, to assume that Matthew's vocabulary and style were different from Q's. However, when we look at the QC words, we find a fair number of striking phrases (e.g., "there shall be weeping and gnashing of teeth," "you offspring of vipers," "O you of little faith!") and even whole sentences which come once in the QC material as well as several times in Matthew. So it would seem that Matthew's and Q's styles were similar, and there is a self-contradiction in the International Q Project.

Kloppenborg makes a second and surprising mistake in suggesting a difficulty for the FGH. Matthew has added most of his Q material into his basic Markan structure, usually at suitable contexts. Luke virtually never agrees in putting the new material in these same contexts. How can this be explained, Kloppenborg asks, if Luke was rewriting Matthew, as claimed by the FGH? Actually, Kloppenborg and I have the same answer to this question. Luke also has a basic Markan outline, and he works to a simple technique. He copies Mark from Luke 4:31 to 6:19, from 8:4 to 9:50, and again from 18:15 to the end. With the limitations of ancient copying facilities, this was the only sensible procedure. In between he takes up Matthew, leaving out any matter also in Mark; so all

---

5. M. D. Goulder, "Self-Contradiction in the IQP?" *Journal of Biblical Literature* 118 (1999): 506–17.

the new material falls automatically in the non-Markan sections. There is no problem; and Kloppenborg explains the order of Luke in exactly the same way, save that he thinks Luke used Q for the non-Markan blocks where I think he used Matthew.

It may be suitable to add a final word on nonrational reasons for preferring one or another solution. Kloppenborg is surely right about this. People prefer the 2DH because it gives access to an early view of Jesus, or because they were taught it by a revered teacher, or because they do not have time to read the recent literature, or for many other reasons. I have every reason to try to diminish the force of these nonrational considerations; and one such recurs in Kloppenborg's essay, though not, I think, intentionally. A number of times he mentions the FGH as having few adherents or of my bemoaning this; and I should not wish my reader to be left with the impression that I am a complaining maverick! In fact I am encouraged by the speed with which the FGH has come to be seen as a challenger to the 2DH. Kloppenborg's citations from Harnack and Marxsen testify to the confidence of the 2DH, and it has not been difficult for it to brush off the Griesbachians. In the 1990s two books on Q by British authors Christopher Tuckett and David Catchpole opened with lengthy defenses of the 2DH against me, and Ronald Piper, in a survey, noted the lapse of confidence in Great Britain. In a new commentary on Matthew in Danish, Møgens Müller writes, "The Achilles' heel of the Two Document Hypothesis is the so-called Minor Agreements."[6] I do not think that democratic voting can solve the Synoptic Problem, but in the long run the best theory not only has to win the argument but also to overcome nonrational resistance.

Response to Robert Derrenbacker

I much appreciate Robert Derrenbacker's careful and courteous critique of my work and will try briefly to respond to his challenges.

Regarding tables: The New Testament communities were familiar with tables (lit., four legs) for eating and for banking: a bank was (and still

---

6. M. Müller, *Kommentar til Matthaeusevangeliet* (Dansk Kommentar til det Nye Testamente 3; Aarhus: Aarhus Universitetsforlag, 2000), 37.

is) called *trapeza* in Greek. The financier stacked money on a table, and receipts and IOUs were written on such tables. Matthew was sitting in his tax booth at the receipt of custom, and the unjust steward says to the debtor, "Sit down quickly and take your bill and write." So people were perfectly used to writing at tables. The copying of texts was done by slaves, often by dictation, and a master might not wish to waste money on his slave's comfort; but the absence of pictures of the ancients writing at tables does not at all prove that they totally lacked imagination or preferred to be uncomfortable.

I may be wrong about tables, but if I am, it does not much affect my theory: Luke can balance his scroll of Matthew on his left knee and copy or amend it in his own text on his right knee. But what about Derrenbacker's Luke? He has no table, and he is conflating his copy of Q with his copy of L (or Mark), as well as writing his own scroll; will he not need three knees?

Regarding reverse order gleaning: Derrenbacker makes several objections to my hypothesis of Luke's gleaning of Matt 16–23 by going over the chapters backward; but I do not think they are too damaging. It is not a complicated operation to follow one version of a passage while recalling another; in almost any sermon one may hear the preacher expounding the lesson read from the Gospel, but slipping from time to time into one of the parallel Gospel versions. Naturally s/he will tend to recall the more striking or memorable alternatives; so it is not surprising if Luke has Matt 16 open in front of him, but recalls the more impressive version from Matt 24. The ancients were familiar with reverse-order exposition. The first poem to Lamentations in *Lamentations Rabbah* goes through Lam 1:1–22 in backward order from 1:22 to 1:1. Nor is there much technical difficulty involved. Our earliest papyrus texts of the Gospels, 𝔓66, for example, are divided by ektheses; that is, a unit like the good Samaritan is marked in the text by a line with a letter sticking out as the unit ends, probably to signal to a lector in church that the unit is finishing.[7] Such markers would enable Luke to pick out one Matthean pericope from another in a moment.

---

7. For reference to this phenomenon, see Eric G. Turner, *Greek Manuscripts of the Ancient World* (Princeton: Princeton University Press, 1971).

Response to Gary Gilbert

I feel very flattered by the seriousness with which Gary Gilbert treats my first book and its discussion of the peoples in Acts 2. He raises an interesting question on Luke's intentions in giving the list of fifteen names; it is always a pleasure to have a consensus challenged. He certainly makes a good case for Roman lists of provinces as symbolic of imperial greatness; and it may be that he is right in seeing a Christian version of this in Tertullian. But I have some hesitations about his proposal that Luke had such a "spiritual empire" in mind:

1. Luke tells us that the Jews living in Jerusalem had come there "from every nation under heaven"; and no doubt, as an educated man, he had heard of India, Britain, and Ethiopia. If the aim was to impress the reader with the worldwide extent of the kingdom of God, should we not expect such places to be named? Of course Luke might not know of Jews living in India or Britain; but he does know of Jews living in Ethiopia, Syria, and Greece, and he is likely to have heard of them in Spain, Gaul, and Italy. But, in fact, of the fifteen names he gives, fourteen fall within a circle a little over a thousand miles in radius from Jerusalem. Only Rome is further than this. Five fall round the Fertile Crescent (Parthia, Media, Elam, Mesopotamia, Judea); five in modern Turkey (Cappadocia, Pontus, Asia, Phrygia, Pamphylia); and two in Africa (Egypt and Cyrenaica). Then there is Rome, the world capital and the bourn of Luke's story, and the appended Crete and Arabia back into the circle.

2. The geographical limits of the list certainly suggest an older world, such as that which Gilbert cites from Isa 11 or I (and others) from Gen 10. The order and balance of the peoples is a bit like Gen 10, too. Shem is the senior son of Noah, and the five mostly Semitic peoples come first. Then comes Japhet, and the Iapetic peoples are mostly in Anatolia; Jews called Greece *javan*, but the word comes from Ionia, "eastern Greece," now roughly the Roman province of Asia. Last come the Hamites, where they belong, and only two of them. I no longer think that we should deny the Cretans and

Arabians to Luke, since they are in every manuscript — he is just plugging the gaps.

3. So where does this leave the question of Luke's intentions? I think Gilbert is right to be suspicious of the prophetic-return theory. At the most we could say this is a foreshadowing; Luke, like Paul, saw Jewish rejection of the gospel as the opportunity for the Gentiles, but he probably also saw the whole Jewish people coming into the church in the fullness of time. But Luke is so respectful to the empire, with its fair-minded administrators, that it is difficult to see him offering a spiritual competition. Perhaps the reversal of Babel, so often understood of Acts 2, suggests that there is something in the Gen 10–11 link after all.

Response to Alan Segal

Alan Segal wrote a most interesting book, *Two Powers in Heaven*,[8] which I read soon after it came out; it was among a cluster of books, beginning with Christopher Rowland's *Open Heaven*,[9] that opened my eyes to the importance of Jewish visionary literature, and Segal and I became comrades in arms. Perhaps our common feeling for "dry English wit" helped this. The same insight, developed from the same background, is to be seen in many of the comments he makes in his essay (though I do not share his enthusiasm for Fletcher-Louis). But for all that I have learned from him on the topic, we are not at one on its application to Paul, and I felt that this was the Achilles' heel of his more famous (and widely praised) book *Paul the Convert*.[10] There is not leisure here to comment on so full an essay, and the best I can hope is to take the two visionary passages which Segal appeals to and to argue that their context shows them both to be hostile to the visionary movement in the church.

---

8. A. F. Segal, *Two Powers in Heaven: Early Rabbinic Reports about Christianity and Gnosticism* (Leiden: Brill, 1977).

9. C. Rowland, *The Open Heaven: A Study of Apocalyptic in Judaism and Early Christianity* (New York: Crossroad, 1982).

10. A. F. Segal, *Paul the Convert: The Apostolate and Apostasy of Saul the Pharisee* (New Haven: Yale University Press, 1990).

First, then, a distinction is made between a revelation and a vision. Paul's own experiences are always described as revelations (*apokalypsis*). This is what happened when he was converted (Gal 1:12), though he had seen Christ then (1 Cor 9:1); it was by revelation that he went up to sort out the observance of food laws by Gentiles (Gal 2:2), and he had many such revelations (2 Cor 12:7–9). A vision (*optasia*), in the tradition current by the first century, involved being carried up to heaven to behold the throne (*merkabah*) of God. It is such experiences that are being discussed in 2 Cor 12, in which a Christian known to Paul was, about 41 c.e., "ravished to the third heaven, or paradise." These were alternative names for the topmost heaven (later there were seven, and more).[11]

The classic cases of such a vision of the glory of God was that of Moses, though God comes half way to meet him, in the cloud on Sinai (Exod 24:18). This experience, with its elaborations in Exod 33–34, is the topic of 2 Cor 3, Segal's first text; but what he misses is the strong element of contrast in 3:1–4:6. Some new missionaries have arrived in Corinth, bearing letters. Paul calls them "letters of commendation" to diminish them; but in fact they were letters of authorization from the Jerusalem leadership, empowering them to take over Paul's Achaean churches. The Greek terms for authorization, *hikanos, hikanotēs, hikanoō*, are used repeatedly in the next few verses. Such an authorization from the metropolitan church would be threat enough; but in addition, the context implies the claim by somebody to have had visions like Moses and to have been transformed like him.

A key element in the discussion is that Paul does everything he can to put the Moses claim down. His was a ministry of death, of condemnation, written on stone (suitably!), and the glory on Moses' face was passing away — in fact Moses put the veil on his face only to stop the Israelites from seeing the end of what was passing away! Anyhow Moses' glory was nothing compared to that of the new ministry, that of the Spirit, of righteousness, of permanence. So it does not seem very likely that Paul is boosting claims of his own to be following in Moses' footsteps.

---

11. C. R. A. Morray-Jones, "Paradise Revisited (2 Cor. 12:1–12): The Jewish Mystical Background of Paul's Apostolate," *Harvard Theological Review* 86 (1993): 177–217, 265–92.

It is the new missionaries who are making such claims, and as they are unfalsifiable they are a major threat. I am not surprised that Paul does what he can to weaken them.

But of course they are part of the treasury of Scripture, and Paul, as so often, exploits his opponents' strengths by taking them more spiritually. In the nature of the case the vision of the throne was only for the few; so Paul counters, "But we *all.*" The heavenly vision is open in another way to every Christian. We do not need veils and all that, and we do not have access to the highest heaven; but we see the divine glory in a kind of mirror, and we are transformed from glory to glory. What we have seen is the face of Jesus Christ, which is the glory of God and his image. We do not need haloes; what matters is the growth in the life of the Spirit.

The same polemical situation underlies 2 Cor 10–12. The new missionaries (11:4, 22) have been saying that Paul is not a true man of the Spirit. He is not an impressive personality, and he is not a good speaker. He writes these strong letters, but he has not the courage to come and visit the church. His mission is too big for him to service it; he cannot impose proper discipline; he is not a proper, dignified figure, but is always in trouble with the authorities. After two chapters of answering all this, Paul says, "I have to boast: it is no use, but I will come to visions and revelations." It has been part of the attack on his lack of the Spirit that he was thought to be a failure here too. As with many of the preceding charges, Paul can only defend himself ("boast"), and that will not do much good. It is easy to see why these things were said: Paul did not talk about his religious experiences — apart from this chapter we hear of only two "revelations": his conversion, and when he suddenly saw that it was crucial to talk to the Jerusalem leaders about food laws.

The two topics raise very different feelings in Paul. He has never had a vision of rapture to heaven, and he senses that claims to such are usually unhealthy; revelations, on the other hand, he has often had, and he is indignant at the reproach. But first he deals with the harder point, and like many a man in a corner, he takes the offensive: "I know a man in Christ who, fourteen years ago — whether in the body I know not, or out of the body I know not — God knows — that such a man was ravished to the third heaven. And I know that such a man, whether in the body or apart from the body I know not — God knows — that he was ravished to paradise, and heard unspeakable words, which it is not permitted for a man to utter." The repetition is a sure sign of Paul's impatience with the pretentiousness of the whole topic. People claim to have these ravishings and sit discussing whether they took their bodies to heaven with them! We sense a slightly bad-tempered feel to Paul's account, rather as when in Gal 2 he is talking of the Jerusalem leaders "claiming to be something," and he says that means nothing to him — God is no respecter of persons.

This leads on then into a second attack: Paul's friend heard "unspeakable" speakings, which it is "not permitted for a man to utter." When a negative is expressed twice like this, it is usually a sign that someone else is saying the opposite (cf. 1 Tim 6:17: "[God] who only dwells in light unapproachable, whom no man has seen or can see"). We know from Col 2:18 that some Jewish Christians made use of their visions to manipulate church opinion, and in Judaism mystics were allowed to report what the angels sang (i.e., God's praises), but not what they said. So the force of Paul's response in 2 Cor 12:1–5 is a straightforward counterattack. It is true, says Paul, that I have never been ravished to heaven, but I have a friend who was, and very differently from these new missionaries; he did not talk grandly about whether he had taken his body with him, and he kept his mouth shut about what he had heard — unlike these people who blab out forbidden secrets.

Paul ends the discussion with what seems a translucent contrast: "On behalf of such a man I will boast, but on my own behalf I will not boast, except in my weaknesses." He could in fact boast truthfully about his many revelations, but he will not because he does not want to puff himself up (12:6); but he will boast about "such a man," the modest, restrained Christian who had been taken up to see the throne. I really do not see how Segal can say, "The change of person from third to first gives me the clear impression that Paul is speaking of himself." Surely the change of person implies a firm contrast between two different people.

Response to Krister Stendahl

How gracious of the doyen of American New Testament scholarship to attend the symposium, a man who has achieved the highest positions and reputation in both church and academy. And how particularly gracious is his final sentence, using words that would do for my epitaph: "Not a perfect pearl, but a pearl nonetheless."

INDEX OF
ANCIENT TEXTS

APOCRYPHA AND PSEUDEPIGRAPHA

INDEX OF
AUTHORS AND SUBJECTS